One Word but Many Tongues

Confessions of a Multiculturalist

Matthew J. Motyka

Hamilton Books

An Imprint of
Rowman & Littlefield
Lanham • Boulder • New York • Toronto • Plymouth, UK

Copyright © 2017 by Hamilton Books
4501 Forbes Boulevard, Suite 200, Lanham, Maryland 20706
Hamilton Books Acquisitions Department (301) 459-3366

Unit A, Whitacre Mews, 26-34 Stannary Street,
London SE11 4AB, United Kingdom

All rights reserved
Printed in the United States of America
British Library Cataloguing in Publication Information Available

Library of Congress Control Number: 2016952941
ISBN: 978-0-7618-6846-0 (pbk : alk. paper)—ISBN: 978-0-7618-6847-7 (electronic)

∞™ The paper used in this publication meets the minimum requirements of American National Standard for Information Sciences Permanence of Paper for Printed Library Materials, ANSI/NISO Z39.48-1992.

To my parents,
whose commitment to the Catholic faith
has paved my way to religious life:

Janina and Mieczysław

Brothers and Sisters:
Boasting is necessary, though it is not profitable; but I will go on to visions and revelations of the Lord. I know a man in Christ who fourteen years ago—whether in the body I do not know, or out of the body I do not know, God knows—such a man was caught up to the third heaven. And I know how such a man—whether in the body or apart from the body I do not know, God knows— was caught up into Paradise and heard inexpressible words, which a man is not permitted to speak. On behalf of such a man I will boast; but on my own behalf I will not boast, except in regard to my weaknesses.*

*2 Corinthians 12:1-5, *New American Standard Bible* (2002), http://www.biblica.com/en-us/bible/online-bible/nasb/2-corinthians/12/ (accessed June 15, 2016).

Contents

Acknowledgments		ix
A Note on Translations		xi
Prologue		xiii
1	When Life Was a French Dream	1
2	Outpouring of the Dream into Real Life	9
3	The Dream Becoming Flesh	21
4	Rolling in the Deep	33
5	Saint Louis de Gonzague: Foreshadowing	45
6	San Francisco: New World, New Life	55
7	O Beautiful!	67
8	From Illusion to the Truth	79
9	A Coda: The Idiom of the Human Heart	95
Notes		101
Bibliography		107
Index		111
About the Author		115

Acknowledgments

My foremost gratitude goes to Melinda Erickson who supported this project from its inception to the final version. She tirelessly commented on several versions of the book proposal and subsequent drafts. Without her committed support this book would not have materialized. Moreover, without her assistance regarding my usage of the English language the book would not have reached the level of clarity and readability it shows in its final version.

I owe much gratitude as well to Timothy Wolcott who helped edit the first drafts and whose interest in language, learning, and teaching I share. His encouragement regarding the topic and assistance with English were very much appreciated in the writing process of the book.

Stephanie Vandrick offered invaluable comments on the book proposal and encouraged my idea of adopting the genre that blends academic analysis with personal narratives.

I am thankful to Antoni Ucerler, S.J. for providing helpful insight particularly regarding the title. Anna Kidacka read and commented on the few first chapters and encouraged me in her bold manner to pursue the topic.

I am ever grateful to the rector of the Jesuit Community at the University of San Francisco at the time of the manuscript preparation, John Keoplin, S.J. for his generous support of the project. The University of San Francisco granted me a sabbatical semester in Fall 2013 during which I was able to compose the draft of the manuscript at Loyola Marymount University that welcomed me and offered perfect writing conditions.

The copyeditor, Sam Brawand, provided valuable insight regarding the style and content.

Finally, I thank all the persons who are the fabric of this book and, therefore, part of my life, without whom the story could not have been told.

A Note on Translations

Unless otherwise noted, all translations are mine.

Translations for François Villon are from Galway Kinnell's new bilingual edition and translation, *The Poems of François Villon* (London and Hanover, NH: University Press of New England, 1982); for *The Song of Roland* in this text: *The Song of Roland: Translations of the Versions in Assonance and Rhyme of the "Chanson de Roland,"* trans. Joseph J. Duggan and Annalee C. Rejhon (Turnhout, Belgium: Brepols, 2012); for Montaigne, from M.A. Screech, *The Essays of Michel de Montaigne*, (London: Allen Lane, The Penguin Press, 1991); for Jean Racine, *Andromaque*, from http://www.poetryintranslation.com/PITBR/French/Andromache.htm (accessed September 9, 2013); for Plato, *Phaedrus* (c. 370 BC), by Benjamin Jowett is available online at http://www.gutenberg.org/ebooks/1636 (accessed May 14, 2016); for Jaufré Rudel [Joffré Rudel], *The Songs of Jaufré Rudel,* ed. and trans. Rupert T. Pickens (Toronto: Pontifical Institute of Medieval Studies, 1978); for "Letter to Posterity," in *Petrarch: The First Modern Scholar and Man of Letters*, ed. and trans. James Harvey Robinson (New York: G. P. Putnam, 1898); for Torquato Tasso's *Gerusalemmme liberata*, *Jerusalem Delivered: An English Prose Version*, trans. Ralph Nash (Detroit: Wayne State University Press, 1987); for Pierre Corneille's plays, *Seven Plays*, trans. Samuel Solomon (New York: Random House, 1969); and for Henri Michaux's "Ma vie," trans. Valerie Smith and James Bushnik, http://www.reelyredd.com/0605.michaux_ma_vie.htm (accessed May 13, 2016).

Prologue

My life has been marked by continual beginnings, defying the classical notion of beginning, development, and conclusion. At the stage of life that most people are planning for retirement, I was entering the so-called professional world. Plato would have despised me for my lack of specialization, my dilettantism; he would have banished me from his republic as a day dreamer with poetic inclinations. This is who I am—an actor rather than an author. I know nothing of my own but enact received ideas by giving them flesh and blood so that they can be perceived and felt. And this is the essence of the sacramental priesthood: a priest has nothing of his own to offer; he has only a manner that translates something difficult to grasp, a *mystery*. In a homily addressed to priests, Pope Benedict XVI called this mystery the audacity of God "who entrusts himself to human beings—who, conscious of our weaknesses, nonetheless considers men capable of acting and being present in his stead—this audacity of God is the true grandeur concealed in the word 'priesthood.'"[1]

I had not intended to study French. It was given to me as one is presented a bride in a traditional society. I said yes to her obediently, for lack of an alternative. I wanted to flee her several times but never managed to do it. French and its culture have become one with me, as expected in a lifelong marital commitment. We both have known betrayal and extramarital adventures, but reason and the sense of mutual belonging have always had the last word. When the gloom of long working hours as well as the bad Parisian weather altered my moods, I flirted with Spanish. When Spanish rejected my advances by showing its cultural particularity, impenetrable to an outsider, I reconciled with French but then succumbed to the charm of Italian. When the Tuscan standard started making me feel that I would never master perfectly its subtle system of changing stress pattern, I humbly returned home to

French. All was fine until English came along and discretely, but imperialistically, took over my native Polish despite the grammatical and phonetic pitfalls into which I keep falling, even after a quarter of a century. Yet French has had its last word. Unlike the English-Polish symbiosis that has become an unconscious part of me, French has remained a faithful partner, a referent, and a companion with whom I process the intellectual, ethical, and spiritual challenges of my existence.

This book wants to tell the story of my relationship with French that was my guide, my vehicle that brought me out of the houses of bondage. These houses were both the oppressive Poland from before the fall of the Iron Curtain and the deceitful West where I landed, lured by agreeable illusion. French protected me against despair and easy optimism accompanying me faithfully to the gates of freedom within the Jesuit order. In all certainty, I state that I am not one of those people who can claim to be the architect of his own happiness. My happiness is a result of obedience to fate, or providence, whichever you prefer, my potential reader. I have been a passenger on a skiff, tossed about by waves, without a steering gear. Only *mystery* or the audacity of God can explain why I have anchored in this harbor.

Chapter One

When Life Was a French Dream

It is July 1, 2012, and I am in Kraków, Poland traveling to meet some friends with whom my adventure with French began some thirty-five years ago. I am in a car driven by Małgorzata Pieniążek, one of the former students with whom I started college at the Jagiellonian University. As we travel to a restaurant, neither of us is surprised by the ravages of time in our physical appearances. We have seen each other several times since I left Poland in 1981. This will surely not be the case a few minutes later when I greet the people with whom we are dining since I have not seen them since college years. We arrive at our destination, a popular restaurant, and indeed there is a shock. Troubled by the physical change in these friends whom I last saw in their youth, I withdraw for a moment into the imagery of François Villon's poetry, which I studied for the first time in a classroom with them. I suddenly understand Villon's poem, "Ballade des dames du temps jadis" [Ballade of the Ladies of Time Past], that I could not quite comprehend when studying it at nineteen years old. This is one of the best known poems that constitutes part of François Villon's collection *Le Testament* in which the fifteenth-century Parisian poet and adventurer transforms a personal account of his troubled life into a cosmic human experience punctuated by fall, suffering, and redemption.[1] Now I get what Villon meant. "Ou sont ilz, ou, Vierge souveraine? / Mais ou sont les neiges d'antan?" [2] [Where are they, sovereign Virgin? But where are the snows of last winter?].[3] Emotion wells up in my throat. I think to myself, "What happened to your unripe features: où sont les Dames du temps jadis [Where are the Ladies of Time Past]?"

As the conversation unfolds, I realize that they have lived and are now anticipating their retirement. Their physical appearance, betraying fatigue, confirms this anticipation. I listen to their tales of life. They are beautifully fulfilled in a new Poland that is, now, not mine. Our generation just barely made it to the new free-market system, avoiding the bitterness of our parents' generation, who missed out on the benefits and new opportunities that the economic change made available to their children. Our generation's parents had to swallow the bitter pill of seeing the new system, often run by technological advances that they were too old to master. Their children embraced the new system and also benefited from it. They were players in the sociopolitical changes within the Poland of the 1990s and the first decade of the 2000s. And now that they have reached their retirement age, I thought, what do we have in common, in fact? Very little, indeed.

I had been reluctant when Małgorzata suggested a class gathering after all these years. During our conversation, I realize that my friends remember much more from our four years of college together than I do. This may in fact be an alert for me that despite all the beginnings of my life, biological decline is knocking at my door and perhaps my memory may be betraying me. In any case, I justify my lapse in memories by admitting that I have probably had too many unfinished beginnings in my life, and they have superposed themselves in my brain, overshadowing the Polish episode. Yet I am enjoying this encounter after all. It clearly tells me that time has passed and, because I have no children of my own to tell me that I might be a grandfather one of these days, I absorb the aging lesson from the group, who share the pride of being parents of grown children. In fact, the son of one of the reunited classmates, who studies in Kraków, turns up for a few minutes to please his mother by saying hello to her circle of friends. His effort makes it plain that we are more than a bunch of grown-ups.

What do I have in common with this group? French. For me it all started in the first year of high school, not very far from Kraków, in Myślenice, where I first heard "Bonjour." The sonority of it suggested a call from a fairy outside, or, a *call* in the sense of vocation. A call from a reality that must have been very different from the realm of communism. In fact, in the Polish mentality, even after World War II, French culture was perceived as the universal model of good taste in all domains of life. It evoked charm, intelligence, and philosophical wisdom to be found in literary works, most of which were translated into Polish by prominent Polish authors. I had vaguely assimilated that view of Frenchness, but not until that first *bonjour* did I actually feel invited to explore it as a refuge from the overwhelming gloom of a 1970s Poland approaching the limit of its capacity to bear the yoke of Soviet imperialism.

The domination of central Europe by the Soviet Union began during World War II (1939-1945) after the Soviet army (the Red Army), assisted by the Polish army, that had been reorganized on the Soviet territory and under the Soviet control, liberated the region from the German occupation.[4] The winners over Germany—the United States, the United Kingdom, and the Soviet Union—met in February 1945 in Yalta to decide the fate of Germany as well as the liberated countries. The allies conceded the division of post-World War II Europe into two sectors, divided by what would become known as the Iron Curtain, separating Eastern Europe from the West. Poland, because of its geographical location and the maneuvering of Soviet leader Josef Stalin, fell to the Eastern side, to be controlled by Stalin's Soviet Union. This meant a progressive subordination of the country to the Soviet model of governing. Right after the liberation, secret agents started preparing for the implementation of the Communist system by arresting the political opponents of the pro-Soviet political orientation and sending them to concentration camps or simply executing them. The Soviets backed the local Communists who won as a result of corrupt elections in 1947. The new Polish government partially confiscated and redistributed farmland, and also then took control of the mass media and the education system. Subsequently, the Communists either absorbed or seized control of the organizations of civil society: churches, sports, youth groups, trade unions, and farmers' unions. One of the goals of the Soviets was to create a homogeneous Communist society achieved in part by ethnic cleansing. The Polish borders were pushed westward giving Poland part of the former German territory while the Soviet Union annexed considerable parts of the eastern Poland. The population from the eastern territories of the pre-World War II Poland was either displaced to the new western territory or sent to labor camps in Siberia for suspicion of antisocialist attitudes or activities. Later, in the late 1960s, many of the Jews who had survived the Holocaust were forcefully exiled to Israel.

Economically, the new satellite countries of the Soviet Union were compelled to reject the American economic aid known as the Marshall Plan (1948-1952) that helped Western Europe recover from the ravages of the war.[5] The refusal to receive the American assistance was intended to oblige Eastern Europe to rely on the economic assistance from the Soviet Union. As the Communist economy eventually became a complete fiasco, the Soviet Union demanded more and more of the mediocre production taking place in the rest of its block. The economic crisis escalated in the 1970s, particularly with the advent of the 1980 Summer Olympic Games in Moscow, that increased pressure for supplies of food and merchandise. At that time, the Polish movement of the independent trade union federation, eventually known as *Solidarność* [Solidarity], started to emerge as a staunch political player. There had been outbursts of political dissent in Eastern Europe in the past, but normally it was severely repressed by the political police Służba Bezpieczeństwa, widely known by its abbreviation SB, and the army. This time it was to be different. Fewer than ten years later, in 1989, the Eastern Block collapsed nearly without bloodshed.

It was in the economic and political climate of the 1970s, with Poland's severe shortage of goods as well as rising political dissent, that I began my exploration of the French language. I started avidly learning French. Its sounds and meanings projected *an elsewhere* on the barren walls of a Communist classroom that seemed determined to keep young Poles satisfied with the political status quo. For me, the French language triggered a desire for a lightness of being that would allow the self to be oneself. Even though the vast majority of the teachers in Poland were not indoctrinated by the official ideology nor did they try to force us to believe in the system they themselves likely despised, the atmosphere was heavy. The other subjects, such as Polish, did not leave us much room for reflection on individual human needs. Our Polish teacher, Mrs. Koniuszy, loved early nineteenth-century literature, known as Polish romanticism, and focused the class on Poland's struggle for independence during that period. This strategy probably spared us most of the twentieth century's social realism, that lauded the achievements of the Socialist policy in our country. But, the focus on the Polish romantic imagination, informed by uprisings, deportations, and exiles, did foster a feeling of Polish uniqueness. Ultimately I think this national self-perception as a people who has suffered more than the others is a curse for Poles trying to make their place in the world community. This sense of uniqueness among the world nations causes major difficulties for Poles in adapting to cultural otherness outside Poland. Experiencing the lack of understanding of the idiosyncrasy of Polish culture abroad, they oscillate in their attitude between megalomania and the inferiority complex, opting for isolation rather than acceptance of the mainstream culture.

French, on the other hand, manifested itself to me as unapologetically universal. Take, for example, its verbal code of politeness. The Polish custom of greeting can, at best, be seen not only as plain, but also unsophisticated. In Polish, there is nothing like "comment allez-vous?" [How are you], with its expectation of an affirmative answer conveying the best of moods, even if really wishing that the interlocutor of the moment would vanish from the face of the earth. A Pole, unaware of this other social convention, would likely say what was in his or her heart, without perceiving that a truthful answer was not called for. The Polish cultural script, characterized by its sincerity code, ignores the power of sophisticated politeness.[6] It does not admit that a highly codified behavior represents a shield against unwelcome intrusions of an external world that would expose our vulnerability through its unguarded demeanor. A "comment allez-vous?" [How are you] with an answer "je vais très bien" [I'm fine] allows control over the interaction. One may stop the conversation sharply, without offending anyone, or add another question and pursue an exchange if one wishes.

That formality conveyed by the French language helped me, it seems, to structure a social self that my native Polish did not provide. It helped to build a distance between the peer pressure to conform and the desire to preserve a margin of freedom to be oneself. I felt that I could consciously learn new ways of saying things that would set me apart from the collective high school experience. I despised my high school years. There was no room for students' personal development. Students were treated like robots expected to perform programmed functions without any concern for their talents and interests. The assessment focused on the reproduction of the material with no reward for a creative assimilation of the content. French became a methodic attempt to free myself from the mold of the insensitive, collectivist approach of socialist pedagogy. I began to idolize French along with whatever it evoked in me: I pictured myself on the Left Bank browsing stands of the *bouquinistes* or listening to Juliette Gréco somewhere on St. Germain-des-Prés—these were some of the first cultural *clichés* that I absorbed from accounts of French culture.

As my French language proficiency developed, my teacher told me the Institut Français in Kraków, a cultural center operated by the French Consulate to promote French culture and language. It had a library as well as a weekly screening of French films which I started attending. The Institut, which was called Salle de Lecture before rising to the status of an *institut*, was housed in an elegant building in the old city of Kraków, on the street Św. Jana. After climbing the old staircase, I was welcomed by an elegant receptionist—a Polish lady adopting French airs and wearing a distinctively French fragrance. It set her apart from the crowds of tired Polish women on the streets of Kraków, whose main concern was not elegance, but, rather, what to feed their families. Having absorbed a whiff of exquisite French perfume, I would venture into the reading room where I could browse through the colorful issues of *Paris Match*. The extraordinary news of happy people I was getting to know through the gossip-column pages awakened a desire in me, not to become like them (I was not that naive, fortunately), but to see the blue sky of the Mediterranean and its beaches and yachts, from which VIPs communicated their well-being to the world, uncontaminated by the worries of everyday life. Once I had satisfied my curiosity about the lives of my new acquaintances, I would walk to the library, from where the smell of *livres de poche* would emanate and enchant my intellect.

My first encounters with French literature, however, were the translations of Albert Camus, Honoré de Balzac, and Molière, required reading for my Polish course. Camus's *La Peste* [*The Plague*] left the most unforgettable impression on my teenage sensibility. The way the community faced an apocalyptic reality with a collective effort to circumvent its annihilating impact awakened in me a rebellious dimension of my personality that would eventually come to the surface. As the absurdity of the situation in which the inhabitants of Oran in *La Peste* moved the protagonists to act against it, the absurdity of the political state of Poland, due to increasing economic demands of the Soviet Empire, engendered rebellion against this unbearable status quo. The whole of the community was confronting the overpowering, massive wall of imposed passivity that needed to be shaken off. Camus's fictional account shows both heroic attitudes, and cowardly and resigned ones. The Polish population was not immune to these social divisions: there were cowards, heroes, and passive onlookers. Too vulnerable myself, preoccupied by my mother's frail condition, I adopted a passive position. I became an observer, neither cowardly nor heroic, of the situation that climaxed in a military *coup d'état* on December 13, 1981. By then, I was already in France.

However, in my high school years, I withdrew into the shell of the French ideal: its language and literature. I remember devouring, during a summer, Balzac's pages of *Le Père Goriot* in which the ungrateful daughters of the protagonist live lavishly, hiding their modest origin. As I was to discover only a few years later, Paris was a stage on which actors performed the roles they were given by surrendering their bodies and souls to it. They had to discard the traces of their modest origins, just as the Goriot daughters did. The mandate of the Parisian way of speaking was one of the pressures with which a provincial or a foreigner had to wrestle when trying to find a place in the social network of the city. I found myself like Molière's Tartuffe, in a rich household of the French capital, seeking acceptance by the selective Parisian milieu. Like Molière's protagonist, I pretended my assimilation to the city's precious manners until my departure for the city of Berkeley many years later, where I would eventually discover my true self. But, my *self* now had an imprint of the Parisian chapter in my life that would never leave me.

Yet there, in the reading room of the Institut Français, I was both young and innocent enough to succumb to the alterity of the culture that offered a saving alternative to the one that triggered constant discouragement and frustrations. I could sit amid the collection of *livres de poche* and browse freely. At that time, Balzac was difficult for my level of French literacy, as was Molière; however, I avidly read books by André Gide. I could comprehend his prose, with its overly classical style and restrained vocabulary. *L'Immoraliste* intrigued me greatly. It was not so much the question of his marriage to his cousin, Madeleine, but the frankness of his discussion that I found so different from Polish literature, which was committed to social issues and shied away from the type of daring introspection that the French were writing about so boldly.

Once a week the Institut Français showed a French film. The films were either classics or relatively recent productions in which generous nudity, often without cause, and glimpses of dialogue that I could follow offered the main reward for my attendance. Yet a few screenings were truly memorable: *La belle et la bête* [*Beauty and the Beast*], screenplay and direction by Jean Cocteau, was such an event.[7] The beautifully delivered dialogue gratified my longing to understand spoken French. The story had a magical quality that remains with me to this day. The *beautifying* power of love, with its transforming grace, wrestles us out of our *beastly* reality. Further, the magic of the story cajoled and inspired me to find ways to transcend the condition of my birth. It stirred the intuition that started pointing, little-by-little, toward transcendence. In that period transcendence meant to me a rise above the typical condition of a Pole of my age: finishing high school, going to college, finding a sweetheart, getting married, finding a job, and settling within the limits of the modest stability allowed by the Socialist state's economy.

Yet the search for transcendence could not be dissociated from my religious upbringing. My parents were Roman Catholics, as was the majority of the Polish population in the post World War II era. They were not particularly pious, but ascribed to the rituals that being Catholic entailed, that is, they attended Sunday mass and ensured that their child received a religious education. This did require, nevertheless, a dose of heroism on my mother's part. She was a teacher at a public grammar school and, by the time of my confirmation, the school's principal. After a few years as the principal, and about a year after my father's death in August 1970, my mother was dismissed for a perceived close friendship with the pastor: a bad moral example for both the Communist government and the parish.

Until his death my father held the Catholic Church in high esteem. Every night he prayed, ensuring that this act served as an example for me. Quite a few times he explained to me the intentions of his prayers: he was giving thanks for surviving two wars in which he was a soldier, and he prayed for a man whom he accidentally shot on a foggy morning at the border with Belorussia, not having seen that the soldier was surrendering; the man had begged him for prayers before he expired. Then he prayed for the collapse of the Soviet Union and political freedom in Poland, and, finally, for a sudden death without confinement to bed. When Father Chramiec, who was reputed to be a holy man and who had hidden my father in the presbytery for some time during the German occupation, left the parish after many years of ministry, Father Ryznar was missioned to the parish. My father found his preaching of such dismal quality that he started listening to the Vatican mass on Radio Free Europe and avoided attending mass in the parish church. As a result, when he died, some voices were raised that my father should not be buried in the local cemetery because he might not have been a real Christian.

My father's sudden death on a late summer day—in the manner for which he had prayed—was the first brutal irruption of mystery into my rather carefree life. Fear for my mother's health, which was showing signs of deterioration, and my anxiety about becoming an orphan, started to cloud my late childhood years. My mother was diagnosed with a severe form of diabetes and suffered from a degenerative rheumatoid arthritis. I knew I had my faith to cling to without grasping what that really meant. I did not understand for awhile why I was singled out to be a half-orphan at the age of twelve, and the image of God the Father as an almighty and an intransigent ruler paralyzed my whole being. The fear of God, rather than the trust in his kindness, led me to an emotional state that numbed my spiritual life for many years to come. I never doubted that God existed and that he was actively involved in my life, but my religious education had not given me the tools to discern God's discretely leading presence in my life, while instilling in me the perception of the constant threat of retribution for my innate inadequacy. The fear was somewhat reinforced by my father's frequent comments about my predisposition to messiness, which was, according to him, a hereditary trait from my mother's side of the family. He had acquired his Germanic orderliness through his schooling under the Austro-Hungarian Empire in Kraków, and often bragged about it when he was disappointed with my failure to meet his standards.

Yet that numbness, rather than an absence of the Spirit, helped me traverse difficult teenage years during which I witnessed the progressive demise of my mother's health until her death ten years after my father's. It was during that period, the French language entered my life and offered itself as a gate out of the melancholy that had instilled itself in my life since the death of my father. The first "bonjour" uttered by my high school teacher, Ewa Rachwał, awakened me from the lethargy to which I had succumbed. With that *bonjour* the construction of the new *self* was born. Subsequent visits to the Salle de Lecture of the Institut Français consolidated my burgeoning desire to become *un autre* [other].

Chapter Two

Outpouring of the Dream into Real Life

During my last year of high school I resolved to apply to the Jagiellonian University in Kraków majoring in French. The program was somewhat archaically called Romance Philology, but it corresponded broadly to a French major curriculum in other countries. To be admitted to the program, candidates were required to take an entrance exam in the French language, Polish literature, and world history. It was commonly known that the university took only those candidates who had spent some time abroad or who were privately tutored by employees of the Department of Romance Languages. I had done neither, and most of my family advised against my decision, suggesting instead that I use their own connections to get into the Agricultural University [Akademia Rolnicza]. Notwithstanding this intimidating counsel, I was determined to take the entrance exam. To the surprise of many, I was admitted to the program. As I discovered later, my peers were a mixture: mostly daughters of those who could afford a stay abroad—either due to questionable wealth or because of connections with the government—or those who had managed to receive private tutoring with members of the department. And many had, like myself, prepared for the entrance exam on their own, following their local high school teacher's advice. We did it mainly for the sake of French and what it represented for us.

And so it came time to study French, its culture, and literature full time. After a difficult four years of high school, I could finally dedicate most of my time to the study of what I liked. At the university, most of the subjects were taught in lecture halls with about eighty students. We also had discussion groups for most of the subjects. These discussion groups were in fact conducted as seminars for which students were assigned reading. The students' motivation varied. Some of them wanted just to perfect their French to escape to France or Canada. Some of them were very good students and some of them were very good students who excelled at all of the program requirements. Some of them did not appreciate the rigidity of the program and the teaching methodology, but nevertheless enjoyed the subject matter. I found myself in the last category and blamed my lack of a truly scholarly temperament for preventing me from earning the highest scores on exams. Only when I attended school in the United States did I realize that its system better suited my temperament that does not, in fact, tolerate learning by memorization and perfect reproduction of the teacher's output. Processing data, or learning, by writing essays was a liberating feature of the Anglo-Saxon system and allowed me to flourish. But, that liberation came much later.

During the four years at my university in Kraków, I had to comply with the dominant style of teaching and learning. It did give me, I must confess, a broad cultural and historical background that was useful, and still is, in my studies and research in America. Yet, during that time in Poland and a few years later in France, it was a cultural assumption that pleasure should not be associated with learning; learning was meant to be hard work. Students were discouraged from the more personal view about a subject that results from writing an essay. And yet, to the credit of the higher education institution in communist Poland, the amount of freedom the professors had was remarkable. Thanks to their scholarly integrity, we students were exposed to authors whose views had nothing to do with the Communist Party line. Most nineteenth- and twentieth-century French poetry, for example, had no relevance to the Marxist ideology supposedly embraced by our government.

Nonetheless, students were required to take courses in the political economy of socialism and Marxist philosophy. I failed my course in political economy on my first attempt—I could hardly conceive of the superiority of socialist quinquennial planning over a free-market economy while my diabetic mother drilled holes in her arms to inject insulin with *used* needles because of a needle shortage. I memorized the ideological nonsense eventually, and cleared my record on the second attempt. As for Marxist philosophy, teachers organized the curriculum as a survey of Western philosophical currents, and Marxism appeared in it merely as one of the trends. It was a clever strategy to shelter students from indoctrination or from a dislike of philosophy altogether.

The studies in Kraków deepened my relationship with French. The initial attraction of a *bonjour* evolved into an outburst of feelings: a true love affair, a period of *fiançailles* [engagement]. I was happy in spite of the deterioration of the Polish economy, and at the same time, the decline of my mother's health. French literature was inviting me to enter the universe where *moi* was more important than the supposedly egoless political system that turned out to be inhuman, or, as I describe, an ideology that saw humanity as screws in a monstrous tank destined to run over the world. Its loose screws could be tightened or replaced at will by the machinist, unchecked by any bill of human rights.

The basic textbook for our studies of literature was the anthology *Lagarde et Michard*.[1] It provided students with a useful historical background, in addition to excerpts of the canonical works. The anthology was well-suited for the program because it focused on the literary history of France. Since the exams required a great deal of memorization of historical facts, names, and titles, it was most practical to own these textbooks. I acquired the whole anthology through a family acquaintance who lived in France. It cost about half of my mother's disability pension, but having the collection did make my studies much easier.

It is ironic to think that thirty years later we do not even need to buy books to find the information contained in *Lagarde et Michard*—a click on the computer would do. Moreover, the borders between France and Poland have disappeared; today I could simply go from Poland to France to buy the books I needed. But the difficulty then of finding French books has left a mark on me to this day. I always hesitate to write notes on printed materials; I still wrestle with the remnants of the guilt induced by the purchase of the *Lagarde et Michard* collection.

But *Lagarde et Michard* was the diamond ring that sealed my covenant with French and its culture. Reading excerpts from *Lagarde et Michard* improved my reading proficiency. Afterwards, I could extend my reading interests at the Institut Français where now I could look for the *textes intégraux* [complete versions] by the authors of the excerpts included in the collection as well as those mentioned by the professors in lectures.

Our course in French literature was chronological: it started with the oldest period, the Middle Ages. This might not have been the best idea because the medieval vernacular was Old French, an almost different language, and most students were still in the process of becoming fluent in Modern French. Reading Old French texts without a modern translation was simply impossible. The language barrier remains one of the reasons that fewer people choose to specialize in medieval than, for example, twentieth-century literature. Thus, my full appreciation for the quality of medieval literature had to wait for some years until I enrolled in a course on Old French language and literature with Professor Howard Bloch at the University of California, Berkeley. Systematic reading and the study of the language helped reveal the fullness of the human experience woven into a literary fabric that married the sublime with the scabrous in the way that modern and postmodern aesthetics cannot withstand. Modern attempts would be subjected to either censoring incisions or audacious labels. In that distant period, audacity was the norm in popular culture.

Despite my linguistic limitations, in Kraków I received a preview of what the Middle Ages must have been like. We read *The Song of Roland* from a

Larousse edition that contained major sections of the work. I recall being surprised by studying God's intervention in the camp of the Christian Franks fighting the Moorish army in the Pyrenees in the ambush set by the traitor knight Ganelon. Then, I was irritated by Roland's proud refusal to blow the horn to bring help from the main Christian camp led by Charlemagne. His heroic death could have been avoided if he had listened to the wise advice of his companion Olivier and had blown the horn:

> Dist Oliviers: "Paien unt grand esforz,
> De noz Franceis m'i semblet aveir mult poi;
> Cumpaign Rolands, kar sunez vostre corn,
> Si l'orrat Carles, si returnerat l'ost."
> Respunt Rollant: "Jo fereie que fols,
> En dulce France en perdreie mun los."[2]

> [Says Oliver: The pagans have a great force;
> it seems to me our French are very few.
> Companion Roland, sound your horn
> and Charles will hear it, the army will return."
> Replies Roland: "I would be acting like a fool!
> In sweet France I would lose my reputation."][3]

The work stirred some atavistic impulses in me, reminding me that bold and blind heroic attitudes, typical of the Polish ethos, do not always pay off, nor did they in the numerous Polish insurrections of the nineteenth and twentieth centuries. And the exaltation of heroism that French culture has abandoned, particularly since the tragedy of France's involvement in World War I, which resulted in over a million casualties, echoed strongly in my mind. My sensibility was fed by my father's tales about his own deeds in the two world wars. Based on his stories, I assumed that he would have readily related to the ambushed Roland's sacrifice on the battlefield near Roncenvalles in Northern Spain, but I was not convinced that heroic sacrifice was the best possible solution to the conflict. I wondered, were these thoughts just a sign of rebellion against my very Polish father? The loss of my father at an early age interrupted the development of the father-son relationship, and it needed a resolution.

I knew I was not going to be a war hero like my father, or a revolutionary. The emergence of the Solidarność [Solidarity] union while I was a student in Kraków offered such an opportunity to test my political abilities. While supporting and cheering for the dissent against the Communist Party line, I did not become a militant. On one hand, I was too concerned with my mother's declining health. On the other hand, there was something in me that did not like any form of political involvement that blinded one's perception of reality. Once, I went to a meeting of the students who were actively involved in the rising opposition; I looked at their faces and listened to their speeches and saw that their whole being was under some sort of spell. At that time I did not know exactly what to make of this. Now, from the experience of many encounters of that sort, I can say that it was the *spell* of ideology. Political life needs an ideological simplification of reality, regardless of its orientation. Liberation movements want to liberate the people by arming them with accusatory ammunition against the oppressing Other. Conservative movements want to protect people from self-doubt by urging them to adhere to the framework of tradition. I had too many doubts about myself and did not want to place the responsibility for my weaknesses on the government, or on someone else. I sensed that there was more to human existence than politics, important as it is for shaping the way we live.

What was it in me that generated a drive for living in spite of the hopelessness of the political outlook in Poland, before it underwent radical political changes? The economic situation in Poland progressively deteriorated to the point that one could only buy food almost exclusively on the black market or through the governmental rationing of meat and sugar. Thanks to my mother's resourcefulness acquired in her teens during the German occupation, we never went without food. Only once did I stand in line to buy a smelly chicken in exchange for a government coupon. While I stood there, I thought there must be more to life than bad politics that lead to an economic situation whereby people are reduced to the primitive condition of fighting for food. French culture, with its sense of aesthetics, reinforced the feeling that sometimes, in fact, the grass *is* greener elsewhere; or at least, fresh green grass is available somewhere without having to cross barbed wire walls to reach it. It was while waiting in that line that I decided to leave Poland for good if a chance presented itself.

While acquiring that old smelly chicken, the poetry of François Villon came to mind and shed some consoling rays on our common human fate. We read in our literature course "La ballade des pendus" [Ballad of the Hanged Men] in which the fifteenth century's genial poetic voice begs for compassion:

>Freres humains qui après nous vivez
>N'ayez les cuers contre nous endurcis
>Car, se pitié de nous povres avez
>Dieu en aura plus tost de vous mercis
>Vous nous voiez cy attachez cinq, six
>Quant de la char que trop avons nourrie
>Elle est pieça devoree et pourrie
>Et nous les os devenons cendre et pouldre
>De nostre mal personne ne s'enrie
>Mais priez Dieu que tous nous vueille absouldre. [4]

> [Brother humans who live after us
> Don't let your hearts harden against us
> For if you have pity on wretches like us
> More likely God will show mercy to you
> You see us five, six, hanging here
> As for the flesh we loved too well
> A while ago it was eaten and has rotted away
> And we the bones turn to ashes and dust
> Let no one make us the butt of jokes
> But pray God that he absolve us all.][5]

At that time I wanted the solidarity of all the *freres humains* who would understand my predicament living in a place that did not have much joy to offer. Villon provided me with a universalist perspective on human suffering that went beyond Poland's borders. Suffering appeared to me to be an inherent part of the human condition. Before reading Villon, I lived somewhat under the spell of messianism that underlies the Polish culture: we suffer, and because of that, we have a special messianic role under the sun. It is a heresy that legitimates a dangerous megalomania grounded in the loss of past imperial ambitions. At the time of this first encounter with Villon's poetry, of course, I could not have anticipated that one day I would be a chaplain saying masses on death row at San Quentin State Prison in California, or that death's vicinity would cause the same shiver in my being at the sight of dead men walking and begging for a glimpse of compassion: "Freres humains … [n]'ayez les cuers contre nous endurcis."

The first semester's literature program compressed the first three centuries of French literary history. After *The Song of Roland* and Villon, we dwelt on Jean Racine's *Andromaque*. After the fall of Troy, the title character Andromache, the wife of Hector whom Achilles has slayed in a duel, is taken prisoner by Pyrrhus who is madly in love with her. Andromache is, however, staunchly committed to honoring her husband's memory and to shielding her son Astyanax from political intrigues. After a period of interior conflict, she opts for a compromise by accepting Pyrrhus's advances assuring thus the safety for her son whose life would have been in danger had she refused to comply with Pyrrhus's demands.

> Mais son [le fils d'Hector] fils périssait: il l'a fallu défendre.
> Pyrrhus en m'épousant s'en déclare l'appui;
> Il suffit: je veux bien m'en reposer sur lui.
> Je sais quel est Pyrrhus. Violent, mais sincère,
> …
> Je vais donc, puisqu'il faut que je me sacrifie,
> Assurer à Pyrrhus le reste de ma vie;
> Je vais, en recevant sa foi sur les autels,
> L'engager à mon fils par des noeuds immortels.[6]

[Yet my son dies: he must be protected.
Pyrrhus by wedding me will act for him.
It is enough: I place my trust in him.
I know this Pyrrhus. Violent, but sincere,
...
I go then, since I must be sacrificed,
To give to Pyrrhus what is left of life;
I go to hear his vows at the altar,
And bind him to my son all the deeper,][7]

The power of the play resonated in my inner being: a widowed mother trying to protect her son from the dangers of a world that was just waiting to abuse them both. It could have been my fate if my mother had not used all of her enterprising skills to maneuver through the world of men—one of whom took advantage of the remnants of her youth, and when these faded away, retained her as a house attendant and cook. And she complied, just as Andromaque had done for her son, Astyanax, in order to protect him from the Greeks. Andromaque's character's plight helped me understand my mother's inner conflict—a widow trapped between an unconquerable passion and the maternal instinct to ensure there would be a decent future for her son by providing for his education.

I reached my second year of studies, after which I would be required to spend the summer in a three-week language immersion camp in a student residence in Kraków, led by instructors and organizers of cultural activities from France. The residence hall, Nawojka, became an island of Frenchness for all college students in Poland who finished their second year of French study (or as it was called, "Romanistyka"). There were perhaps 200 of us; some students came willingly, others were forced. One could be exempt from the immersion camp if one had an opportunity to go to France that summer. Most of us did not. The only group that was forced to come were three female students from the Katolicki Uniwersytet Lubelski [Catholic University of Lublin], the only Catholic institution in Poland that survived the suppression of Catholic schooling after World War II. To my surprise, they had nearly native proficiency in French and were ostentatiously arrogant toward us, the mere products of the Polish state school system. They wore expensive and revealing clothes that matched the audacity of their verbal contempt for the surroundings in which they were placed for three weeks. They took advantage of their advanced language proficiency to engage in more intimate conversations and relationships with the French staff than we possibly could, or would dare. And I thought, "Is that the school for which we have contributed to periodic collections in our parish church?" I advised my mother that in the future we should save some expense on that work of mercy.

All things considered, the French summer program in Kraków met all my expectations. The French staff who came had full awareness of and sensitivity to our situation in Poland, where the economic situation was degrading from month to month. Most of them learned the expression "nie ma," which means, roughly, "out of stock," or more literally, "we do not have it." This was the typical answer in any store where one would try to purchase food.

But in Nawojka we ate relatively well for three weeks. During the day we had language classes and in the afternoon we participated in cultural activities and workshops. In the evening there was our social life, animated by the French staff members. Generally it was going to a discotheque. The most memorable experience for me was dancing with Paule, one of the teachers who came to Kraków with her husband, Jean. He could easily have been her father. They were a very loving couple, but Paule did like dancing with younger Polish men. Dancing with Paule was like a conversation in a language that one has not mastered fully. It was a series of attempted communications through embraces, and indicated a longing for liberation from a fate that had crippled us in our drive to fly beyond physical and moral limitations. Paule was beautiful, in her late twenties, of Corsican origin, tall and tanned, moving her body gracefully, and letting her long black hair fly freely around her shoulders.

I also made friends with two "Normaliens," Rémy Parain and Guillaume Roger, students of the Ecole Normale Supérieure at Saint-Cloud, a suburb of Paris. This elitist institution was meant to prepare the brightest minds of the nation to become teachers at the French state universities and high schools. At our age of twenty, they were already *fonctionnaires d'état* [state employees] with a monthly salary paid by the French government until their retirement. Of course, to reach that level, they had to sacrifice their teenage years by studying like programmed robots in order to pass a national *concours*, an entrance examination that has the reputation of being the most difficult challenge in one's life. Among the alumni of this republican system, France produced Jean-Paul Sartre and Simone de Beauvoir.

That summer the two Normaliens came to Kraków for adventure and also to experience for themselves the reality of the communist system. The political climate at the Ecole Normale was dominated by sympathy toward the socialist system. It diffused claims that the poor economic situation in countries of the Soviet bloc was largely fabricated by enemies of progress in the West. It was an eye opener for the two young Frenchmen, who soon realized that the system did not function according to the principles of Marxist political economy, as it claimed to. With one of the Normaliens, Rémy, I have developed a lifelong friendship; I try to see him and his family as regularly as the distance between Europe and the United States allows. When I settled in France for nearly a decade in the 1980s, the assistance of his family was essential.

But during that summer in Nawojka, our two worlds came together. On one hand, this cultural exchange strengthened our hopes for a change in

Poland. On the other hand, for the French, the encounter brought about the realization that in other parts of the world people kept admiring the French ideals of freedom and democracy as the universal principles to which all nations should aspire.

After the summer living at Nawojka, the world no longer looked the same. It became more and more difficult to live in a gray landscape where the shortage of basic goods was the national topic of conversation. Like bullfighting, or soccer in Hispanic countries, competition for toilet paper, toothpaste, and white sugar became the topic of conversation in the workplace. Moreover, these were workplaces where nobody actually worked, because even the supervisors were involved in the food hunt and often left the office to stand in line at markets.

Equally scarce were medicines. When my mother's arthritis became very painful, my French connection happened to be very useful. Reluctantly, I asked one of the Normaliens, Rémy, for help acquiring Voltaren, an anti-inflammatory drug that was impossible to find on the Polish market. His family generously responded to the request and supplied my mother with the medication for the next two years, practically until her death in May 1981.

Amid the turmoil of the political situation and of my mother's health issues, I was offered an opportunity to travel to France. Each year the French government provided scholarships to Polish students to attend a summer study abroad program in Grenoble, my university being the recipient of seven. Traditionally, the best students and those supported by people of influence were admitted to the program. I did not think I would qualify, since I did not think I belonged in the first category and was sure that I would not find anyone influential to support me or influence the selection on my behalf. And yet, as a sign of the times, the student leader and representative, Maryla Gawron, a woman of unusual moral strength and integrity, stood up and eliminated most of the people who, in previous years, would have benefited from the protection of their Communist Party network. Maryla made her selection—perhaps not completely based on scholarly merits but also on the potential for having fun on the road—and had it approved by the university. I made the cut.

Before hitting the road to the West, we had a few months of study during which we were expected to select a topic for our master's thesis. After a long hesitation, I chose a director who was reputed to push her students toward the completion of their projects. She suggested as a topic, "Onirism in Gérard de Nerval's Writings," an early nineteenth-century writer whose associative poetic manner foreshadows the technique of the surrealist movement of the twentieth century. I liked reading Nerval's *Les filles du feu*[8] ["Daughters of Fire"], a collection of short stories whose title characters are young women. The best known of these stories is *Sylvie*. The collection constitutes a series of reminiscences of women he met in his life. The representations are wrapped in the dreamlike atmosphere portraying protagonists as fairy beings emanating a subtle eroticism. The dance described in *Sylvie* made me think of dancing with Paule: a dance that was more than a dance. It was a search for a new reality or surrealism that would camouflage the daily struggle, transcending what did not appear to have much sense: life as I saw it. For me, as for Nerval, dance would become transcendence itself. In addition to Nerval's fiction, his own tragic life, marked by progressive madness that ended in 1855 with his suicide, made him an even more attractive subject of study. He composed a dozen sonnets titled as a collection *Les Chimères*. They abound in hermetic, symbolic imagery that lends itself to diverse interpretations. The sonnet "El Desdichado" ["The Wretch"] resonated in my ears with a strange despair. I heard in it a soul mate whose life was escaping him on a trajectory with no specific destination.

> Dans la nuit du tombeau, toi qui m'as consolé,
> Rends-moi le Pausilippe et la mer d'Italie,
> La *fleur* qui plaisait tant à mon coeur désolé,
> Et la treille où le pampre à la rose s'allie.
>
> [You who consoled me, in the tombstone night,
> Bring back my Posillipo, the Italian sea,
> The *flower* that so pleased my wasted heart,
> And the arbour where the vine and rose agree.][9]

Obviously I had never seen Posillipo, a residential quarter of Naples, but the poem kindled a kind of atavistic nostalgia in me to see the deep blue of the Mediterranean Sea and also a desire to forget the inhospitable winter of Central Europe, both climatic and economic. I was to discover the color of the Italian seas near Venice in a few months while travelling through Northern Italy to Grenoble.

The year went by quickly, and, in the Spring of 1980 as I started to prepare for the trip, I heard from the two Normaliens. They were returning as staff members for the French language immersion program in Nawojka. We would miss each other because my stay in Grenoble coincided with the workshop in Kraków. Of course, even the extent of my gratitude for the medication that my mother received throughout the year did not outweigh my desire to see that *distant elsewhere*. Moreover, our train itinerary included Vienna, Venice, and Milan. In Venice, and later on a day-trip from Grenoble to Nice, I would eventually see that sea of Italy, the Mediterranean, that has exercised ever since an attraction over me that even the majestic Pacific of California cannot overshadow. I made arrangements for my mother to thank her benefactor in person— a meeting between my mother and Rémy, which was quite moving for both. As they reported to me, they communicated in German quite effectively. My mother was to live about nine months after the meeting with Rémy.

The time for the trip to Grenoble came. It was probably the most amusing time of my life. Six of us were traveling together. We laughed often and anything could be a trigger: the guards at the Czech frontier, the order of Vienna's streets, the jovial interaction of Italians, and even one of our companions hiding under the train seat in order to cross the French border. It was a laughter we used to disguise our tension over the drama back in Poland that was about to explode—a confrontation between the Polish working class and the government. The political situation in Poland was reaching a climactic point as labor strikes and citizen protests were taking place. Once in Grenoble, we saw pictures from the shipyards in Gdansk showing crowds openly protesting the government. In Poland, we could not have seen these pictures, obviously. On my way back to Poland, I smuggled in a few issues of *Paris Match*, a French weekly magazine covering international and political news. These issues, containing sensational photographs of the protests, were later circulated among family and friends.

One of the participants of the program was a daughter of a highly placed security serviceman. She was planted among us to supervise the group. Fortunately, she was not a Mata Hari and swiftly got romantically involved with North African men who provided pleasure and a promise of marriage. A promise they kept until the last day of our stay and then vanished from the surface of the earth. At the conclusion of the Grenoble adventure, I and the other male participants were conscripted to carry the heavy suitcases of the brokenhearted, which she had filled up with capitalist goods. We carried them until we arrived in Venice, where we too conspired and vanished within the narrow streets of the lovely city. She made it back home on her own.

But what about the first encounter between the dreamed of and real France? The South of France delivered the promise of beauty and charm. Grenoble was a relatively calm city with a large university campus occupied mostly by foreigners during the summer. A visit in Nice, Cannes, and Monaco fulfilled all the visual expectations we had regarding this legendary part of France. What was missing in our experience were the native French. They all had gone on vacation in August, incredible as it seemed. We interacted mainly with foreigners who had come to Grenoble to study or perfect their French language skills. The most noticeable and engaging was a group of Chinese who wore revolutionary uniforms and spoke French impressively. There was also a group from the Soviet Union whose members, although not in uniforms, interacted reluctantly with outsiders. Only once did I get into a heated discussion at the cafeteria with a Soviet female student who wanted to smack me in the name of the Western freedom I defended. She called us in very good French ungrateful Polish bastards who forgot who liberated Poland from the German occupation.

Although our visit to Grenoble did not provide a satisfactory French experience, it strengthened my determination to move to France one day. I knew that if I did immigrate, I would likely move to the north of the country, near or in Paris, where the employment possibilities were greater than they were in the beautiful south, and also where people with whom I was acquainted lived. Returning to Poland, my fresh enthusiasm for life, lit by my experience abroad, was soon extinguished. I found that my mother had changed physically during my five-week absence. She whispered to me that the doctor discovered something alarming in her body that might require surgery. Ultimately the surgery became needless; the cancer spread to her liver in a matter of a few weeks. She passed away in May 1981.

It was a difficult year with many demands. It was the year I was required to pass all my exams if I was to submit my thesis on Nerval the following year. The thesis did not go very far. I decided to postpone it until the next year. The most urgent concern was my exams. There was a comprehensive French language proficiency exam, two literature exams, and a historical grammar exam. The next concern was to estimate my mother's longevity. If she lived beyond the summer, I would need to stay in Poland and would miss the opportunity to return to France. If she died in the middle of the academic year, I would have to deal with several issues regarding my housing and the completion of the academic year. As it happened, she died toward the end of the semester, after I had passed all my exams.

The political situation in Poland was becoming more alarming. Polish television began regularly showing the maneuvers of the military forces of the Warsaw Pact.[10] I received the draft notice to join the Polish Army in the upcoming January. I entrusted our house to the practical intelligence of my very resourceful aunt, one of my mother's sisters. It was possible to travel outside Poland; however, the waiting period to obtain a passport was long. My aunt had access to the local police (*milicja*) commander whom she had to bribe several times for deliveries of regular supplies of fodder for her poultry farm. We then filled an envelope with dollars bought on the black market and went to see the commander. I vaguely remember a repulsive, sleazy male figure, rather short, speaking to us indirectly and stressing the great effort it would take him to accelerate the process of issuing my passport. I swallowed my pride in order to obtain my goal, but I walked out of that office resolute that this was the last time I would abase myself to that extent, even though these methods were effective and normal in the Polish system of that period. Six weeks later my passport was ready. On July 29, 1981, I was on my journey out of Poland, forever. Once in Paris, a multifaceted guilt would occasionally seize me and dissipate only through a prayer for forgiveness, offered in gratitude for allowing me to make that leap to freedom in the realm of French, a freedom that had its price as well.

Chapter Three

The Dream Becoming Flesh

The intimate experience of my mother's physical decay and ultimate death left me with the feeling of guilty relief when I eventually found myself free to do with my life as I pleased. But there was little time for reflection on these conflicting feelings. When considering an initial place to stay in Paris I did not want to abuse the generosity of the Parisian family, who had supplied my mother with Voltaren medication. With that, I wrote to a French couple whom I had met by chance in Kraków and who invited me to spend a month in their apartment if I needed a place to stay. Thus, I had a landing place for a few weeks. I was afraid of flying for the first time, but the thought of not leaving Poland made me recover my composure quickly. I coordinated my flight with a fellow student, Iwona Tobjasz, who had an *au pair* summer job in Versailles. We landed on July 29, on a beautiful day, with a limpid blue sky. Parisian sunlight hurt I vividly recall, my eyes not used to such abundant luminosity. We decided to go to Montmartre since Iwona was due in Versailles only in the evening, and I planned to call the French couple in the afternoon to announce to my arrival. The view of the white stone of the Sacré-Coeur visually melted by the intense rays of the sun with the cooling blue of the sky above transported me completely. "Yes, this is the city where I will try to make my home," I thought. We ate our baguette with cheese on the stairs of Montmartre and contemplated the metropolis which was to be my home for nearly a decade. Iwona returned to Poland after two years urged by her mother who could hardly cope with the separation.

This first day in Paris was a moment of intense enchantment; an overwhelming euphoria that could be stirred by the encounter with the bride one knows only from pictures and people's accounts and descriptions. From the top of the Butte de Montmartre I carefully observed the expanse of this new physical presence that, on that sunny day, offered all that it had to entice the eye of the first-time beholder. Former dreams and new reality blurred in a joyous vision of the new beginning sealed by a determined hope to make my home in the bosom of this free city.

I had brought only two hundred dollars with me for the whole adventure. If my acquaintances could not receive me, I could stay in a hotel, maybe for one night. Fortunately, when I called them I was invited to come to the couple's apartment in the Quartier Latin on the street Pot de Fer. I got there just in time for an offer of dinner on the patio. Asked how I was, I replied "exténué" [exhausted], the answer giving me a reputation of a very "posh" speaker of French. Indeed, I was praised for my mastery of French even though I had a clearly noticeable Slavic accent. Yet having learned French from literary texts, many of which were from the nineteeth century, I conveyed an aura of erudition. The stress on grammatical accuracy at the University of Kraków gave me a great deal of confidence in uttering long and grammatically sophisticated sentences, a feature that was difficult to convert when I undertook to wrestle with English years later.

As a veteran language teacher I believe liberalization of the foreign language curriculum has certainly enhanced foreign language pedagogy. The communicative method has made it possible to emphasize the early practical use of the language without complete mastery of its grammatical intricacies. Nevertheless, excessive laxity regarding form puts students at a disadvantage professionally. If I had not had a superior grammatical mastery of French, I would not have been employable in France. Even though my accent betrayed a foreign origin, my way of speaking commanded respect, if not admiration. Among Polish circles within Paris, a common joke was the story of a Polish tourist in a Parisian restaurant ordering beef by onomatopoeia "moo, moo," a perfectly sound communicative strategy, though without the likelihood of a professional career in any francophone context.

A few glasses of wine made me forget my state of *exténué*, particularly after I was told that I could stay in the room of the couple's roommate who was away for four weeks. I did not have to worry for a month about where to sleep, just time enough to become familiar with Paris, France, and its culture. Here I was in the bosom of the mythical reality of which I had dreamt for years, and that had been my imaginary refuge from the dreary reality of a socalled socialist economy. The street, Pot de Fer, was located in the heart of the Latin Quarter, just a few blocks from the metro station Monge. It was indeed one of the most picturesque village-like neighborhoods of Paris. Numerous markets *en plein-air*, restaurants, and cafés communicated the celebrated *joie de vivre* throughout the neighborhood. The next day I discovered *millefeuille* pastry in the *boulangerie*; it was very reminiscent of the Polish *kremówka* my mother used to bake: a creamy, rich yellowish filling inside puff pastry. The discovery of the *millefeuille* bridged, unexpectedly, my childhood in Poland with my early adulthood in France. In fact, puff pastry is called in Polish French pastry (*ciasto francuskie*). I felt as if my Parisian bride offered me a similar pastry to my mother's in order to make me feel at home in my new environment. I perceived it as a gift from Paris to encourage my first clumsy steps to become her permanent resident.

As the first week of my life in Paris passed by, a sense of difference began to cloud the enthusiastic impression of my first *tête-à-tête* with the reality I dreamed of while in Poland. Difference reclaimed its rights, showing me little by little that it would take a long time to undo my identity formed in very different circumstances from those in a Western democracy. Signs of difference were like pinpricks whose accumulation led to a state of irritability. The differences were bombarding me from all sides, including the way people dressed, ate, thought, and spoke. What initially was an appealing novelty, soon became a challenge when I realized that I had to adopt it as my way of being to function successfully in this forest of new symbolic forms. Food and dress were minor issues, compared with thinking and speaking. In my efforts to build new relationships, I stumbled while trying to decode the symbolic content of people's utterances and to anticipate their reactions. As Claire Kramsch, in *The Multilingual Subject*, has pointed out, symbolic forms are both conventional, because they "refer to and represent the social and psychological reality of a speech community,"[1] and highly idiosyncratic, containing the inflection of the conventional content with the infused unique personal experience. In my case, my symbolic reality had been constructed in the network of symbols, having no political resonance in Paris. Moreover, the shared part of my symbolic reality with the Poles of my generation was marked by a very particular experience that constituted my uniqueness, my own world of symbols. When at the conclusion of that first summer away from Poland, I began longing for a more intimate relationship with the mythical reality I had woven while in my homeland. As it started brutally unraveling, it left me prey to a sense of solitude and alienation.

The first symptoms of unyielding difference appeared in my relationship with my hosts, Catherine and François. They were generous but both fiercely independent, displaying signs of a relationship that was a mystery to me. In Poland, a couple seemed to be happy together and they showed some indications of oneness. Here, Catherine was clearly interested in her career as a translator. She was preparing for an entrance examination to a school for interpreters and translators. François had his own interests it seemed, being often away. Catherine looked at me inquisitively, and with a sort of growing frustration. She said she loved my being openly neurotic in a very Slavic way, so different from the French controlled demeanor. I had no idea that being neurotic could be a compliment, but here it was apparently so. Was my neurosis a consequence of the Polish stiff courtesy code, or somehow the repressiveness of Catholicism, or perhaps a result of having grown up as an only child? Or, maybe a little of all? Was it nature or nurture? Or maybe it was just my underlying preoccupation with a very uncertain future, a future that had to be addressed?

My sense of difference was soon amplified by encounters with many visitors to the apartment on Pot de Fer during my short stay. One of them was Carol, an American Jew, who was a very independent woman and had come to Paris to write. She was very casually dressed for her age, I thought; she was about fifty, dressed in jeans, and wore her long hair falling freely on her shoulders, choices that in Poland only a twenty-something could allow herself to do. A fifty-something woman was condemned to look like a matron with a tightly fixed bun. Carol and I sympathized immediately even though she was a communist in her convictions. In fact, she was the first communist as well as the first Jew I had met. Given the Polish experiment with socialism, I thought that people in free democracies would learn from that experiment and reject it as impracticable. As we were taught at school, Poland was only in the socialist phase of its ineluctable and irrevocable ascent toward communism which, according to the Marxist theory, was the culminating point of the progress of humanity. Soon was I to find out how wrong I was.

Meanwhile, Carol, my communist friend, wanted to support me and offered me a job as her *homme de ménage* [janitor]. We had a very long conversation in which she unveiled her scruples as a communist about employing someone else to clean her house instead of doing it herself. Eventually I helped to dissipate these misgivings by telling her that it would be a chance for me to gain some financial independence. She was always very generous; she paid me double the amount we had agreed upon. The apartment was indeed very neglected. I cleaned it thoroughly, realizing that I was gaining more than remuneration. The encounter with Carol shed a new light on the complexity of the relationship between Jews and Catholics in Poland.

One day Carol initiated a frank conversation on the issue of anti-Semitism. She simply asked me if I was an anti-Semite. I had no idea what that meant precisely. She was the first to tell me about the reputation of Poles as anti-Semites. Indeed, in my family the Jewish question was never really discussed. In my father's war stories, however, he often discussed the figure of a Jewish doctor in the army. My father spoke of him with fondness describing him as a comical character speaking with a Yiddish accent, and having the skill of buying the best available food from villagers during the military campaign. Of course, I heard of the Holocaust, in the shadow of learning about a romantic involvement of my godfather (my mother's brother) with a Jewish woman. He escorted her to the southern frontier of Poland so that she could escape to Romania and then to the West. He never heard from her again. I recall one event my parents discussed with a dose of embarrassment. I heard them complaining that the best dentist in town was forced to immigrate to Israel in 1968 due to a political campaign against the Jews. Otherwise, the Jewish question never really emerged for me. Carol's question sensitized me to the problem, leading me to view and think about the Polish-Jewish relationship with a new awareness.

Carol, thus was my first employer and the work helped me preserve the meager savings I had brought with me from Poland. In addition to working as Carol's *homme de ménage*, I took an assignment with a Portuguese cleaning enterprise that badly needed employees for the month of August, when many of their regular workers went back home to Portugal for vacation. I was also quickly hired to clean the United Nations Educational, Scientific and Cultural Organization (UNESCO) offices for a month, in Paris's fifteenth *arrondissement*. These two jobs made me appreciate immigrant labor in Paris. I admired the resourcefulness of the Portuguese community, who gained a monopoly on housekeeping business in the French capital. One night, my female coworkers invited me for a Portuguese dinner.. They lived in the *chambres de bonne* [maid's quarters] on the sixth floor of a building in a wealthy neighborhood. The evening was dominated by songs by Linda de Suza, their idol, who, after becoming pregnant, emigrated from her village in Portugal to France, bringing with her only a cardboard suitcase. She soon started a successful singing career in France, a career that created opportunity for her emancipation. The evening brought about anxiety about my own future in France. Would I live like these women and cherish nostalgically my Polish heritage on the sixth floor of a beautiful building? The answer was clearly, "No." Either I would integrate into the mainstream culture, or I would return to Poland if I decided that I could not live without the comfort and familiarity of my homeland and culture.

Yet the growing awareness of difference made me sympathize with another close friend of Catherine and François's, Sophie. Because she was of Russian descent, I felt an immediate ethnic affinity. In fact, she was of White Russian descent, very proud indeed of her ancestry. The label White Russian refers to those Russians who opposed the Bolshevik Revolution in 1917 and often emigrated to the West after Lenin's government took over. Embodying the reputation of the White Russians in Paris, Sophie was very eccentric. Each time she paid a visit to the house, she brought marijuana with her and the apartment filled with smoke. One night all present in the house were forced to sit in a circle and the joint passed around. Perhaps because of my asthma condition, I did not inhale properly; the joint had no effect on me whatsoever. Moreover, I did not quite appreciate sharing one cigarette with six people.

Sophie had a generosity of soul that the French did not show. She was an incredible spender. Catherine told me Sophie could spend all of her wages in one night. She would become very emotional when talking about her grandfather, a White Russian army general, who became a taxi driver in Paris after escaping the Bolshevik Revolution in Russia. Despite this debasement, after work the family would lead a life of Russian aristocrats, which meant drinking champagne in crystal glasses, listening to music, and dancing until the dawn. Sophie carried on the traditions, and yet she had communist sympathies. I could not quite understand how it was possible, but maybe communism helped her to be who she was, a cultural anomaly, not representative of the French bourgeois mainstream by any means. Nevertheless, I thought she was a friend of the household because she was even more neurotic than I on the scale of open neurosis. All these characteristics of Sophie's personality and behavior would find resonances in Polish culture: excess, generosity, lack of discipline, abuse of alcohol, and complicated human relationships.

Here was not my abstract France, but the incarnate reality with its human contradictions: pathetic and fearful; jealous of its glorious past, and in denial of its emerging social economic difficulties. In that August 1981 I felt as if I saw the real face of a bride who had been promised to me as well as depicted in most exciting accounts by skillful messengers, poets, novelists, painters, singers, and filmmakers. How was my betrothed in reality? Was she beautiful? She sure was. The Quartier Latin emanated the enchantment of perennial *bonne vie* expressed through its cafés, restaurants, narrow streets, squares, and markets, inundated by masses of tourists who wanted to catch a glimpse of that *qualité de vie* that they could not find in their native places.

Now, however, my construct had to be checked with the physicality of the bride. How much was I capable of sustaining the image I had created of her? In those four weeks I discovered that I had to transform my relationship to Paris and to France completely or return to Poland without realizing the dream that had sustained me for so long. The decision to stay and foresee a life in France required a deep personal transformation. I was not going to change Paris; I had to do a great deal of work on myself in order to fit into the Parisian tuxedo of a proper bridegroom. The first step was to shed my social economic habits acquired in a *socialist* system that had made me passive toward life. In a new free market situation, I had to change my lack of initiative that came from years of enduring life in a hopeless communist reality. I had to become proactive to survive. Capitalism, moderate as it was in its French version, required, however, watchfulness and an inner drive that I did not possess. I knew that these changes would not happen automatically. It took me a few years to transition from socialist passivity to a greater awareness of my inner enterprising resourcefulness. The face-to-face encounter with France told me I would have a very steep learning curve to adjust to the demands of a so-called free Western world. I had been cheated by life so far by the brainwashing empire of socialist propaganda. Even though nobody believed the communist propaganda in Poland, it infiltrated people's lives like a disease, an epidemic that required periods of treatment and of convalescence.

The prospect of mandatory military service somewhere at the frontier with the Soviet Union sobered my nostalgia about my life of a malcontent dreamer in a Poland that was nearing a major political crisis. After all, I was free in France to do what I wanted to a much greater extent than it would be possible in Poland. If I had gone back to Poland in 1981, my fate would have been sealed for a year and beyond because history now reveals that the country suffered a dramatic period then. The military coup by General Jarezulski on December 13, 1981, squelched the expansion of the free labor union *Solidarność*. My decision to stay in France ultimately protected me from the hardship the Polish people suffered for the next decade until the fall of the Iron Curtain in 1989. Nevertheless, the decision to remain in France did not guarantee immediate prosperity. In Poland, after my military service, I might have eventually become a high school French teacher. In France, the only thing I knew was the French language—not an original asset in a country of almost sixty million inhabitants who knew French at least as well as I, and also had better professional qualifications. But in France, I was free to do with my life as I pleased.

Fear of an uncertain future whispered many outlandish ideas to me. Possibly, I could search for opportunities and use to my benefit the assets of my youth, my inexperience, and my supposed neurosis that the French found attractive. Since I did not have my immediate family nearby, nobody would be directly concerned or affected if I did something absolutely unimaginable, such as committing a crime, even a murder, or suicide. I was free, free like Meursault in Albert Camus's *L'Étranger* [The Stranger] or Lafcadio in André Gide's *Les Caves du Vatican*.[2] Both of these characters commit murder without a clear motive, possibly to test the limits of their personal freedom in the midst of the social conventions that externally regulate their lives. There were places in Paris that could provide background for any number of unruly acts. But I could not commit an *acte gratuit* by challenging social conventions, as did Meursault or Lafcadio. I was an incorrigible Catholic with a Protestant-like commitment for duty, mixed with a Polish snobbism for noble actions. All these *qualities* excluded any truly debase options. I could not kill because the seventh commandment had resonated vividly in my ears ever since my first communion. I could not live off my charm because my parents had kept repeating that youth and the charm that comes with it are fleeting goods. One had to not only use one's talents but also maximize them rather than to live off of one's dilettantish appeal. Finally, my parents inculcated in me a Polish distaste for physical labor by frequent warning that if I earned mediocre grades, I would be good for nothing more than a shovel. It took me many years before I understood and appreciated people making their living by using tools such as a shovel. The prejudice helped me, nevertheless, to resolve to pursue my university studies. The Sorbonne exercised an enchantment that responded to my aversion to ending up as a *ditch digger*.

The emotional baggage of my culture and my religious upbringing was the motivation for my choice to stay in France, for better or worse. The choice sealed by my unshakable hope, the fruit of my cultural heritage, and likely, infused by the mysterious breath that was always with me when the light of optimism was about to be extinguished. During the third week of my stay on Pot de Fer street, Catherine was showing more impatience in talking with me, a sign to look for another place to stay while beginning my life in France. I phoned my Normalien acquaintance Rémy Parain. He had been aware of my presence in Paris and responded very generously. The last time we had seen each other was two years before in Kraków. When he had met my mother the following year, she gave him some an envelope with dollars bought on the black market to reimburse him for the medication. At that time the Polish currency, zloty, was not easily convertible to Western currencies on the legal market, and Rémy would have had little or no use of it. He had kept the envelope all this time and at our first reunion in France he handed it to me. This unexpected action would sustain me during the beginning stages of my adaptation to the Parisian ways. When I told him that my intention was to stay in France, he did not hide that he thought it would be a difficult transition, yet he offered all his support. He was at the point of preparing the notorious French national exams, *concours*, or *agrégation*. He planned to live in the school's residence in Saint-Cloud, a suburb of Paris, and his flat in Paris would be empty. Thus I could live there for the next two semesters. This happy coincidence solved my crucial housing concern for the upcoming year.

The encounter with Rémy, and more importantly, his friendship have been crucial for my relationship with French culture. He introduced me to his family who became a surrogate family for me, especially since I could not go back to Poland. It would not be until the fall of the Iron Curtain in 1989 that I was permitted to return. The Parain family members were practicing Catholics, an anomaly in the France of the 1980s. Rémy's Catholicism was clearly more liberal than mine, less fearful of imperfection, and almost entirely void of scrupulosity. There was a Gallic ingredient in it ready to call for the dispensation of rules whenever possible. I soon observed that the French were much more accommodating in the matter of faith than they were in the matter of politics and economics. In everyday life they were intransigent with a motto "je suis désolé, c'est la règle" [I'm sorry, that's the rule]. In religious matters, they were eager to bend "la règle." Lengthy discussions with Rémy on religion and faith have always been for me a great source of inspiration and continue to this day. At the time of my Parisian beginnings, my somewhat stilted Catholicism was revived by posing the questions that required readjustments of my catechetical reasoning.

Once my immediate living situation had been solved, I needed to extend my French visa to be able to stay legally in the country. The simplest way to have my visa approved was to enroll at a university and obtain a student visa. Iwona and another classmate from Kraków, Anna Kidacka, who had also fled and had a summer job as an *au pair*, joined me in this venture. We found that we had to break through a vicious circle to obtain a student visa. We were attracted by the Université Paris-Sorbonne (Paris IV), the old Sorbonne. In the 1960s, the university of Paris was divided into several smaller units within Paris and its suburbs. Paris IV had the reputation of most closely continuing the character of the old Sorbonne. For a foreign ear, unaware of the internal politics of French higher education, the name Sorbonne carried a legendary aura. In actuality, Paris IV had the reputation of an old uncreative institution with old-fashioned, inaccessible professors who lectured in big lecture halls to a completely disengaged student body. But in September 1981, this did not matter. To become a student we needed a visa, a *carte de séjour*. The university administration told us to return to Poland and then to request a student visa at the French Consulate. The request was obviously unrealistic; if we returned we would not have been allowed to leave Poland. On the other hand, the Prefecture of Paris[3] would give us a *carte de séjour* if we were enrolled at the university. In the process of dealing with the Sorbonne's administration we met with student unions representatives who assisted us with of our predicament.

The process of obtaining our *cartes de séjour* had some interesting twists. The student union that was willing to help us was the l'Union nationale des étudiants de France–Indépendante et démocratique (UNEF-ID). The union was neither independent nor particularly democratic. Its leadership was Trotskyist in its political orientation. It was fascinating to listen to a chain of dogmatic discourse emanating from the mouths of its activists. They wanted education for all, without any restriction or concern for the expense. UNEF-ID and the three of us, Iwona, Anna, and me, became odd allies in our common confrontation with the administration of the Sorbonne. The union promised us help, provided we would participate in its political activities. We went to several *meetings* at which we were introduced as Polish students fighting for change in Stalinist Poland, or more importantly to them, genuine communists with a strong desire for political change. We would collect money for different student activists who were imprisoned in different parts of the world, some of them in Czechoslovakia. Finally, in compensation for our efforts, the union suggested that we establish residency in the Prefecture of Nanterre, a location that was run by a communist mayor and where UNEF-ID had considerable influence. We all managed to find addresses in the jurisdiction of the Prefecture of Nanterre. And, yes, we received our *carte de séjour* which we proudly brandished in front of a very hostile employee of Paris IV, Madame B. Then, she had no other choice but to allow us to register for the fall term that was just about to start in mid-October 1981. When I returned to see Madame B. with my transcripts from the Jagiellonian University in Kraków, she asked me if they were photocopies. Later on, when I needed my transcripts from the Sorbonne, I was told that my transcripts had never been filed. Ultimately, this never mattered. I reminisced about this episode on the day of my graduation from the University of California–Berkeley thinking of that expression, "Success *is* the best revenge."

Our *carte de séjour* was valid for three months. In the meantime, however, the military coup of General Jeruzelski took place on December 13, 1981, and all Polish citizens who found themselves in the French territories were automatically allowed to apply for a work permit. We could then loosen our ties with UNEF-ID, because, paradoxically, the martial law in Poland, which inflicted a great deal of hardship on the Poles in the country, played in our favor.

These few months in France altered my Manichean perception of the world. I started realizing that what was good and bad from a Polish perspective did not apply on the same terms to the French reality. I was expecting the French authorities to receive me with open arms as well as allow me to pursue my studies at the Sorbonne. This did not happen. I did not want assistance from a Trotskyist student union because of my prejudice against anything coming out from the Soviet Union or Russia, but UNEF-ID was in fact my official benefactor at the beginning of my French life. There was no clear correspondence between political categories and labels used in Poland and France. Possibly, had they been born in Poland, those Trotskyist students in Paris would have been fighting the Polish government. Further, state employees such as Madame B. would have been apparatchiks in the state system on the other side of the Iron Curtain.

As in the case of my political views, the experience of meeting French students, particularly the UNEF-ID activists who detested and despised religion, in particular the Catholic Church, led me to some doubts about my religious upbringing. Since religion was not the center of life for my generation in France, with the notable exception of Rémy, I started considering that Catholicism in Poland thrived because of the Church's clever recuperation of the nationalist cause in its struggle against Soviet domination. From the very beginning of the communist government in Poland, the Catholic Church sided with all who opposed the pro-Soviet politics. This attitude, that rallied all the forces of opposition to the Soviet interference in Polish national affairs, gave the Church in Poland a popularity unmatched elsewhere. Church service attendance was very high, bringing in those who were not necessarily motivated by spiritual concerns but, rather, by nationalism that found its haven in the parishes. My doubt fed on this realization—that the union of the Polish national aspirations with the universalist outlook of the Catholic Church might have been the driving force of the popularity of the Church in Poland. Perhaps the only truth to our existence, I thought, was a universal confusion on which the powerful and cunning imposed a semblance of coherence and maintained the status quo by fooling people into an ideological dream, a famous "opium of the people" as Marx had it.

Nevertheless, unlike many Poles whose religiosity did not withstand the test of the new cultural perspective and whose rejection was total, my faith survived despite the test of culture and dramatic political change. There was something visceral in it that could not be washed away by a wave of new ideology, nor by new social practices that could easily dislodge *it* from my center. Looking back, I now suppose I had been touched— chosen by the mysterious presence that has never left me. It was love I think, love on a deep level, a parental type of love that must have come over me when my parents' disability and subsequent deaths diminished my sense of comfort and security. That mysterious presence had put France and its culture in charge of mediating the extent of that Love. Leaving Poland was like leaving the family hearth in order to establish the independence of adulthood. France was the new home, not a motherland, but rather like a spousal domain with her owner's formed identity expecting me conform to her customs and habits.

My attraction to French culture and its language was as a mediator, something of a Virgil or a Beatrice figure in Dante's *Divine Comedy*,[4] that led me out of the forest of the inhibitions that were accumulated during my childhood, into the freedom of self-realization. France stimulated the desire to harness a winged bird of freedom and ride it toward the infinite, away from the constraints of everyday life. Instead of that free ride, France knocked me down and then awakened me from the unreality of my longing. I had to satisfy the requirements of social economic life by taking up its constraints. She refused to be an ideal lover whose gaze would consume my entire being. Rather, she espoused my imperfections by demanding that I accept her as she is and leave behind my dream in which she was the protagonist. During my struggle for my *carte de séjour*, it became very clear to me that I loved abstraction more than any concretization of the ideal. So it was with my human relationships; thus far they had always disappointed me. France grounded me and, instead of a secluded *locus amoenous* [pleasant place], Ovid's idyllic setting where lovers abandon themselves to their passion, offered, through her generosity, a family hearth. At this time in France, there was no room there for narcissistic self-fulfillment, but through hospitality and generosity, a new type of love emerged. Through a long process of self-acceptance, I began to see the imprints of grandeur in common humanity and embraced it. Through France's rigor and discipline of social customs I was invited to reform myself. My personal reformation was to last several years and had to overcome obstacles of secularizing fashions and pressures until it reached the boldness of saying yes to the call of religious life.

Chapter Four

Rolling in the Deep

In October I was living in Rémy's apartment, had my *carte de séjour*, and decided to enroll in a program of "licence de Lettres Modernes" [Bachelor of Arts in Modern Literature] at Université Paris-Sorbonne (Paris IV). By choosing this program, I received two years of equivalency for my four years of college in Poland. To earn a *licence*, I would be required to complete three major modules and a minor certificate of Latin language and literature. Two modules had to be chosen from the field of French language and literature; I selected the historical phonetics of French and modern French literature. The third module was optional in the sense that it could be chosen from a subject other than French literature or language; I selected the field of Polish literature. As I was to discover, the university system was quite a puzzle in itself. Each subject had a *cours magistral* [lecture] and *travaux dirigés* [discussion sections]. The *cours magistral* took place in a lecture hall with hundreds of students from all the sections. The *travaux dirigés* (TD) were sections of thirty to forty students and were taught very much like seminar courses in US colleges. Soon I was able to discover that there was no communication between the instructors in charge of TD and the lecturing professor. The rumor had it that to succeed, the best way was to pay close attention to what was happening in TD.

The subject I enjoyed the most was the study of historical phonetics of French with Mademoiselle Hasselman. Who would have thought that this subject, reputed to be one of the most tedious to master, would have any appeal? The reason was Mademoiselle Hasselman herself. A short lady, slightly bending, with a pair of thick glasses, was transformed into a walking dynamo when explaining most intricate phonetic twists from Latin to French. She would always add a brief cultural commentary explaining what the evolution of words revealed to its student. Her favorite expression was "tenir le coup" [hold out, stay the course], which fit so well with her entire demeanor;

she emanated the impression of someone undeterred by any circumstances in her mission to tell people the story of French. Despite the countenance of an Iron Lady, she was the only one among our TD faculty to notice us and to ask us who we were. After the coup d'état in Poland, she also took time to speak to us. It was thanks to her reaching out to us that I passed this module.

Unexpectedly, the French literature module was extremely boring. In TD the students were doing *explications de texte*, commentaries of literary excerpts, a very difficult exercise for non-native speakers of French. It was not so much the matter of language proficiency as it was the question of the cultural inferences that were completely different in people from different backgrounds. Of course we were in France, and cultural diversity was fine as long as it had been assimilated into the imperialist ideal of Frenchness. I strongly resisted this cultural surrender. My grades were mediocre with comments pointing out my "contestable" understanding of the author's intention. For my money, I thought that the French students got it wrong. It seemed to me that the more tedious and conventional *explication de texte* was the higher evaluation the presenter received. We were definitely not praised for originality.

The course that really destroyed, temporarily, any interest I had in literature was a module on modern French literature. It started with Gustave Flaubert's novel *Bouvard et Pécuchet*—a lengthy story of two middle-aged men who meet each other by chance and discover that they both are copyists, an occupation that evokes a lack of originality in the two men's existence.[1] They become friends, and after an unexpected fortune that one of them inherits, they leave Paris for a village in Normandy and begin to explore every branch of human knowledge. They fail in every single attempt to excel at something and ultimately return to copying. Flaubert intentionally wrote this book in a way that was tedious to read, so that the reader might feel the mediocrity of the two men in their attempt to find some excitement in their life. Spending a semester reading and analyzing this book in class did not help elevate our fresh immigrant spirits, but rather the lectures were boring. The students' commentaries were astonishing to us because they reached conclusions from the text which Iwona, Anna, and I would have never considered given our cultural scope. These inferences were not only culturally bound, but also made us feel like aliens in this world of gloom and boredom, accentuated by Flaubert's explicit attempt to make the reader experience the tedium of life and the futility of efforts to rise above it.

The sense of inadequacy that I acquired due to my poor efforts to mimic the imagery of French students, dissipated only years later while in graduate school at the University of California, Berkeley, when I encountered the thoughts and ideas of Claire Kramsch. Her deconstruction of the ideal of the "native speaker" brought the breadth of liberation from the guilt of being a misfit in the Paris IV academic environment. In her later book, *The Multilingual Subject*, Kramsch, following Julia Kristeva, brings forward the notion of "a subject-in-process." [2] It implies a dynamic, never ending process of positioning the self when confronted with the symbolic forms of a given speech community. Kristeva distinguishes two orders that intersect in the process of the emerging subjectivity.[3] One is the order of the semiotic, a pre-verbal phase that encompasses feelings, dreams, and children's fantasies. The second order is the verbal order of the symbolic, characterized by its structured nature that allows the subject to reflect and make linguistic choices. The subject-in-process operates at the intersection of these two orders that influence each other. Kramsch claims that the semiotic realm is the source of the symbolic: it gives the symbolic forms, characteristic of a given speech community, an affective value that finds its expression in their performative use.[4] It took me some fifteen years to realize that my interpretive wrongdoing was conditioned by dreams and fantasies that resulted from my affectivity impacted by a very different environment from that of my French peers. And my symbolic expression received the indelible mark of difference expressed by the teacher as "contestable."

The feeling of insurmountable *otherness* hit us when we reached Chapter 6 of *Bouvard et Pécuchet*. It deals with the revolution of 1848 and has a section on Poland and its struggle for independence from the imperialist powers that had partitioned it in the past century. We could identify with the two Polish immigrants who happen to be in the village where Bouvard and Pécuchet witness a political debate, "La première discussion violente eut pour objet la Pologne. Heurtaux et Bouvard demandaient qu'on la délivrât. M. de Faverges pensait autrement. 'De quel droit irions-nous là-bas? C'était déchaîner l'Europe contre nous. Pas d'imprudence!' Et tout le monde l'approuvant, les deux Polonais se turent"[5] [The first violent discussion was on the subject of Poland. Heurtaux and Bouvard called for its liberation. M. de Faverges took a different view. "What right have we to go there? That would be to let loose Europe against us. No imprudence!" And everybody approving of this, the two Poles held their tongues].[6]

History repeats itself, I thought. This was what my father used to say about France's refusal to defy Hitler in 1939 after he started war with Poland. France hoped that Hitler would content himself with the expansion eastward and leave France alone. And now sitting in that classroom filled with smoke (smoking in lecture halls and classrooms was not only allowed but fashionable), I thought, "who cares what we do in this classroom listening to the stuff that does not intersect with our situation, nor have any impact on our future as immigrants." Flaubert was right about the platitude of human existence in a very French way that our remnants of youthful enthusiasm found unbearable. In our situation, we did not want to hear that all was doomed, nor that life was a series of boring *tableaux* with no joy in it, nor that we would remain, for the rest of our lives, "copyists" of dictations given by bourgeois employers who would prove Flaubert's pessimism to be true.

In the spring semester, the same module required us to study Henri Michaux's *La nuit remue* [*The Night Moves*]. The poem "La Parpue" has stayed with me essentially thanks to a student's *explication de texte* that attempted a psychoanalytical reading. The student pointed out the alliteration of the labial consonant, in particular the "p" as an indicator of the primitive desire, in the poet's return to the premirror stage of a suckling infant.[7] The name of the imaginary animal "parpue" would rime with "pue," meaning "stinks," evoking the mental scent of fecal matter in urgent need of parental attention. The poem is a clever imaginary depiction of a creature containing both fabulous and verisimilar elements. It could illustrate Bouvard and Pécuchet's ridiculous attempts to describe and classify their pseudoscientific findings.

Astute as it might be, the poem and the students' interpretation, the social irrelevance of Michaux's poetry left me cold and uninspired. What do I care about *la parpue*? Why should I care about some bourgeois intellectual's attempt to reform his empty life by fantasizing about his infancy? Michaux's poetic phantasmagoria was generated by a sleepless night, as the title of the collection suggests, possibly induced by hallucinogenic drugs. Our anxiety was real. Our country just suffered an imposition of martial law imposed in Poland on December 13, 1981, only to be suspended a year later and lifted in July 1983. The images from Poland were alarming, showing tanks on streets and beatings by the *milicja* [police]. The mail from Poland was opened, stamped in red "ocenzurowane" [censored], and then resealed in a plastic bag; phone calls were preceded by a statement "this conversation is being monitored."

In the turmoil of the martial law in Poland, with a lack of a clear prospect for the future, the end of the academic year brought new anxiety about how to sustain my studies. Rémy needed to reclaim his apartment in which I was staying. Both Iwona and Anna worked as *au pairs* and recommended that I try it. I first looked for an *au pair* position through the same agency Iwona and Anna found their placements. However, as I discovered, the job was considered to be gender specific: not by chance the full name of the position was "*jeune fille au pair.*" Although I presented myself to be well suited based on the job description, my gender was an insurmountable obstacle. Fortunately, or maybe not, the brother of the woman for whose children Iwona was the *au pair*, needed someone to care for his children. I found my placement as a *garçon au pair* even though, in truth, I was not qualified for it. I did not like children and did not know how to cook.

One of the reasons I was hired was Iwona's recommendation and my grammatically hyper-correct French, but a more compelling reason was that nobody else in this world wanted to work as an *au pair* for this couple. They were both physicians and worked long hours outside of the home. Their two boys, four and six years old, suffered from the absence of their parents and looked on anyone designated to take care of them as a symbol of abandonment. That was also my fate. At our first dinner with the parents the children ignored me completely. The next morning, my first day at work, I had to listen to spasmodic screaming for several hours: "ma maman adorée! ma maman adorée!" Pieces of our first common spaghetti meal reached the ceiling and the rest landed on the floor. After a few weeks of wrestling with an idea of escaping, even to Poland under martial law, I remembered that, after all, I *was* a son of a school principal. I tried to recall how my mother asserted her authority. In general, she just had to glance in a particular way to bring calm and order.

A great difference between the European and American upbringing is that on the Old Continent children must be disciplined, kept in line. This is changing under the influence of the American Big Brother's psychological approaches, but in the Europe of the 1980s, the child was not a prince in the company of adults. The mother of the two brats told me not to hesitate to use my hand if I felt that there was no other means of insuring obedience. She herself had frequent recourse to corporal punishment: more frequently to a *claque* [slap] than to a *fessée* [spanking]. In Poland a *fessée* was much more common whereas a *claque* would be associated with an excess of physical punishment. So, one day, after a lengthy struggle with awaking the boys, getting them dressed, and taking them to school, I resolved to use *fessées* in the future. The next morning when the routine hysteria began, I did what I promised myself. There was a period of shock for all three of us, but the educational outcome was lasting. In the weeks ahead, I needed only to ask "is there anyone in this room who wants a *fessée*?" They dressed swiftly and were ready to go to school when required, and at meals, no more spaghetti appeared on the ceiling! Moreover, on the playground my capacity of being able to administer an effective *fessée* became famous. When a child from the neighborhood tried to bully my protégés, the threat was issued, "we will tell our *garçon au pair*, he will give you a *fessée* and you will see what you will see." I became popular.

There was a toll on my educational success working in a household for two overworked doctors, nevertheless, my studies required attention. I enrolled in another French literature module to finish my *licence* and contacted a professor to be the director of my future *mémoire de maîtrise* [master's thesis]. The module was a slightly more interesting than the one on Flaubert and Michaux. The first semester of this year was on Molière's *Tartuffe, Le Misanthrope,* and *Dom Juan,* and the second semester was on Pierre Choderlos de Laclos's *Les Liaisons dangereuses*.[8] My writing about literature improved, yet, I kept being criticized for "contestable" inferences from the readings that, I understand now, were foreign and culturally incompatible within the narrow context of the Parisian classroom. Should I change the subject matter by leaving French literature and study something else, in spite of all that it had done for me in the dark years of my youth in Poland?

I liked Molière; *Tartuffe* struck an unexpected note in my new context as a *garçon au pair* in Versailles where some of Molière's plays premiered. I was now part of a strange household that exploited me to a considerable extent. I had to show a cheerful expression in this game of dominance. I was appreciated for my pedagogical skills that were, surprisingly, a revelation to me. Growing up as the only child I had little interaction with children. Yet I must have absorbed some of these skills with my teacher mother's milk because how in this world would I have managed this impossible situation? I looked at *Tartuffe* with a kinder perspective than when I read it for the first time in my Polish high school. What do you do when you see others prosper at your expense and you have no power, other than hypocrisy, but to infiltrate their household and live at the same level? I was an impostor in the household of two middle-class doctors; I had no qualifications for the job but was doing it. I pretended that I was satisfied with the situation. I also hid the fact that this new situation did not make it possible for me seriously study. I was free during the day after taking the boys to school but had to be back at four o'clock to collect them. On Wednesdays, I had a twelve-hour shift because there was no school on that day in France. I did not have to work most of my weekends and normally spent time with Iwona, Anna, and others friends. My fragile sanity mandated it. Unlike Tartuffe, I did not try to take advantage of the family. I was not shrewd enough and remained naive, allowing the others take advantage of me. Nevertheless, I my resentment grew because of my situation and, while showing outer politeness toward my employers, I despised them, from the bottom of my heart.

My resentment was echoed when I read the next Molière play, *Le Misanthrope*. It also intensified my feeling of becoming estranged from my cohort of friends. Moving to Versailles alienated me from the group I frequently saw while residing in Paris. I identified with and my mood was influenced by, I believe, the protagonist of the play, Alceste, who destroyed all his relationships by plunging into dire negativity toward any human commerce. One of his famous repartees characterizes well my mood at that time,

> J'entre en une humeur noire, en un chagrin profond,
> Quand je vois vivre entre eux, les hommes comme ils font;
> Je ne trouve, partout, que lâche flatterie,
> Qu'injustice, intérêt, trahison, fourberie;
> Je n'y puis plus tenir, j'enrage, et mon dessein
> Est de rompre en visière à tout le genre humain.[9]

> [I become quite melancholy and deeply grieved to see men behave to each other as they do. Everywhere I find nothing but base flattery, injustice, self-interest, deceit, roguery. I cannot bear it any longer; I am furious; and my intention is to break with all mankind.][10]

My relationship with Rémy was put to the test. After having received so much help from his family, I could hardly bear the idea that I could never possibly repay it. Obviously, there was no question that he would ask or accept any form of repayment. The feelings of guilt and indebtedness brought me down to the level of rejection of all my relationships. I became a misanthrope, looking at the world in the darkest possible color. All was doomed in my mind. Human commerce was but a commerce seeking to take advantage of the situation. Much like Molière's Alceste, I deliberately withdrew from all of my relationships and, with a particularly wicked pleasure, from those people with whom I suspected held genuine concern and care for me. I wanted to be alone, thereby be free to blame everyone else for being a social misfit.

My situation in Versailles actually offered a chance to reflect deeply on the meaning of my strange predicament. Since my mother's death, my life had been a continuous diversion from any profound reflection about where I was going or where I was to go. Versailles represented that cul-de-sac that forced me to look at the void in my life—from which I could either emerge or sink into the abyss that hides behind its walls. It was a year of darkness, a long night that had to be one of the most formative stages of my life. An obsessive poem, titled "Ma vie," read for the course on Michaux's collection of poetry, was resonating in my ears during sleepless nights,

> Tu t'en vas sans moi, ma vie.Tu roules.
> Et moi j'attends encore de faire un pas.
> Tu portes ailleurs la bataille.Tu me désertes ainsi.
> Je ne t'ai jamais suivie. Je ne vois pas clair dans tes offres.
> Le petit peu que je veux, jamais tu ne l'apportes.
> A cause de ce manque, j'aspire à tant.
> A tant de choses, à presque l'infini...
> A cause de ce peu qui manque, que jamais tu n'apportes.[11]

> [You're going someplace without me, my life. You're rolling away.
> And I'm still waiting to make my move.
> You've taken the battle somewhereabandoning me on the way.
> I never followed, I stay. Where you are leading me,I can't plainly see.
> The very little that I want, you never bring to me.
> Because of this emptiness, I want
> So many things, almost the infinite...
> Because of this emptiness, that you never fill.][12]

That was me "rolling in the deep" as the singer Adele would have it.[13] I was alone with my destiny that was now escaping me. What was I lacking in fact? I had food and shelter, I was not homeless. I was healthy enough to bear the challenge that life presented me. But what was that *petit peu* [very little] that I wanted and could not receive from life? At that time I thought I needed peace and time to study, two conditions that I could not afford. This short-term objective that was eluding me was only a screen that obfuscated the object of my desire. I aspired to the infinite without being clearly aware of it. Michaux was right "A cause de ce manque, j'aspire...à presque l'infini." It took many years to grasp the nature of that aspiration. Distracted by a sense of overpowering false values in mainstream culture, I dismissed the idea of seeking the ideal through the lenses of religion. I elected a sinuous path to the infinite marked by posts of secular achievements. That path finally led me to the degree of inner emptiness that could be deadly if not filled by truth. That truth was to manifest itself in the voice calling me to religious life. Yet in my case, the acceptance of that truth required a long process of self-emptying by a direct experience with various cultural substitutes of the truth that secular cultures construct in order to defer the inevitable contact with the ultimate reality of death.

After *Le Misanthrope*, the next reading by Molière was *Dom Juan*. This reading came at the right moment, just as I began to reach the summit of my cynicism, almost enjoying the emptiness of my life, reinforced by my recent self-alienation from everyone I knew. The last target remaining was myself. Dom Juan is a libertine that does not believe in anything. Playing with the feelings of women whom he seduces and then abandons, destroying their reputation and thereby, their possibility of future marriage, gives him ultimate satisfaction. His main target is human affective relationality. He particularly delights in destroying the bonds between betrothed couples by seducing the women and humiliating the men. His libertinage aims to be free of anything that might hinder his sense of freedom, and, for him, love is one of the key obstacles to freedom. I felt an initial attraction to the character who refuses to dwell in the state of longing; on the contrary he is decisive. He acts and has no regrets about anything he has done.

Nevertheless, Dom Juan's encounter in the play with the tomb statue of the Commandant whom he killed, and the subsequent dinner with it at Dom Juan's house, had the impact of shock therapy. The scene produced a shiver of death that awoke me from the self-destructive lethargy in which I found myself. I did not have the strength to turn my life around but felt that I had reached the bottom of my descent into hell. Although I never stopped going to the church, I attended weekly masses only on the principle of Pascal's wager: if God exists, I might gain something by showing up; if he does not, I am not loosing much by giving up an hour of my weekend.[14] Even toward God I felt a cynical obligation to repay the gift of a miserable life. Nonetheless, contemplating the scene of the dinner with the tombstone statue, something *clicked* in me, somewhere deep down in the instinctive sphere of self-defense where the body reacts, ignoring rationalizations of the confused mind. I needed to wake up.

The second wakeup call came unexpectedly from the Sorbonne itself. At the same time I was attending the classes on Molière, I started some preliminary work on my *mémoire de maîtrise*. I selected a professor who was teaching comparative literature at the Sorbonne, Madame Dominique Millet-Gérard. We met at her apartment on the Avenue de Versailles and discussed a possible topic. I did not have any *idée fixe* about what to write, and she suggested a topic on Fyodor Dostoevsky, Georges Bernanos, and Paul Claudel. The working title was "L'Enfance spirituelle dans *L'Eternel mari* de Dostoïevski, *Le Journal d'un curé de campagne* de Bernanos, and *L'Annonce faite à Marie* de Claudel" [Spiritual Childhood in *The Eternal Husband* by Dostoevsky, *The Diary of the Country Priest* by Bernanos, and *The Tidings Brought to Mary* by Claudel]. Even though the *mémoire de maîtrise* was never to materialize, the preliminary work I undertook and the conversations with Professor Millet-Gérard led to a transformation that I believe has led me to the place I am today.

Defining the concept of spiritual childhood in the background of Dom Juan's counter example worked as an antidote to my existential crisis. Dom Juan's sheer cynicism with no traces of innocence, his last-minute conversion, and his death seemed both repulsive and pitiable. The verse of Matthew's Gospel (18:3) that I found while researching the concept of spiritual childhood resonated as an alarm, "Truly I say to you, unless you are converted and become like children, you will not enter the kingdom of heaven."[15] With this in mind I looked at the characters of the adults in the three texts and noticed their difficulties in adjusting to life. In three other texts the children's characters often exhibited more maturity than did their parents. This is certainly true for the little Liza in Dostoyevsky's *The Eternal Husband* who has to deal with her confused family situation: being a biological daughter of her mother's lover, but brought up by her mother's alcoholic husband.[16] In Bernanos's novel, *The Diary of a Country Priest*, the priest represents a character who shines with innocence and absorbs the evil of the villagers. He is an adult but epitomizes spiritual childhood in his openness to the world in its struggle to remain serene in face of his cancer, and also through his unshakable commitment to the values that he has embraced.[17] In Claudel's drama *The Tidings Brought to Mary*, Violaine's character contrasts with her sister Mara who has never mastered the jealousy she felt toward her sister and subsequently lives an earthly life consumed by passions.[18]

I did not understand the impact of these readings at the time but something new entered my existence as I read them. They forced me to divert my focus on my own narcissistic unhappiness and to look at the object of my true desire: the infinite, buried within me because of my convoluted life circumstances. I began to ponder questions that mystified me. What did it really mean to believe? How does one regain a lost childhood in order to enter the kingdom of God? I suspected that there was a stage of fall before regaining lost serenity and innocence. Claudel's play seemed to be hinting at the idea that the loss of childhood must happen and that the secret of happy adulthood is the capacity of its recovery.

The *petit peu* that I wanted at that time was not apparent to me. The academic year went by very quickly. I was ready for neither the exam of the module on French literature nor my *mémoire de maîtrise* that had not gone beyond the stage of an annotated bibliography and outline. One thing was certain, I could not go on working for the family that charged me with the responsibility of raising their children. The children adjusted to me, but the lengthy hours I needed to spend with them in the evening and on Wednesdays, as well as my inability or the impossibility to focus on my studies, made me determined to quit the job. Through an acquaintance, I heard that someone was looking for a manager of a printing shop in Paris. This was a fulltime position consisting of working from 8:30 a.m. to 7:00 p.m. with a one and half hour lunch break. I met the employer, Monsieur Daloze, a man of thirty-something married to a sort of super model working for Christian Dior (indeed I received a bottle of *L'Eau Sauvage* after accepting the offer). However, I had to renounce my studies as a condition of employment. The job was fulltime; Monsieur Daloze (who himself was a college dropout) was adamant about it. After a brief hesitation I opted for the fulltime job. Finally, I had entered into the bourgeois universe of Parisian life.

The printing shop was in the sixteenth *arrondissement* on Avenue Victor Hugo, one of the wealthiest Parisian neighborhoods. With great difficulty, and after using many connections and references of my new employer, I finally found a room in the seventeenth *arrondissement* near the metro station Brochant. Thus I started my true Parisian lifestyle that could be concisely summarized through the French saying "métro, boulot, dodo," or, "metro, work, bed." I called Professor Millet-Gérard to tell her that because of this change in my life I had to quit my studies. She replied that she was sorry to hear it but urged me to remain determined to resume university studies whenever the opportunity presented itself. Her exhortation was extremely meaningful at the moment when I was about to give in to the new lifestyle in which intellectual preoccupations would be a nuisance rather than comfort. I told this to Professor Millet when I contacted her some fifteen years later as I was about to finish my PhD at UC Berkeley.

And yes, I missed the connection with university life. Working fulltime like most Parisians made me discover another side to France that I did not expect. This reality was very much removed from the literary universe I had absorbed through books. Everybody around me was busy working lengthy hours; very few people would know anything about the great works of literature of which they should be proud. The majority would have read some excerpts in high school of the authors whom I thought to be emblematic of the French identity. I was getting settled in a bourgeois pattern of life: a percentage of my salary was paying my retirement fund, the medical insurance (which is less universal than people outside France think; you only receive it if you work), and a five-week per year vacation. I eventually got that *petit peu* that I desperately wanted. To my disenchantment, everyone working in that neighborhood—merchants, store managers, office employees—were going through their routine because it ensured them of *petit peu*, in other words, survival. Bitter, anxious, and often angry, they faithfully pursued their humdrum existence with no idea of rebellion.

I learned quickly how to manage my store. Most of the time I was taking orders for business cards, invitations, and rubber stamps. Occasionally I would make photocopies and bindings for dissertations and brochures. Customers liked me because I was polite and considerate. They were curious asking about the origin of my *petit* accent, and learning its source they usually reacted with a cordial smile. In general, the population of *le seizième*, usually affluent, was very sympathetic to Poland because of its anticommunist standouts. They avoided contact with my boss, Monsieur Daloze, who was often rude in a proverbially Parisian way with no worry of loosing customers. Fridays were more relaxing because Monsieur Daloze would leave early to go to Deauville to play golf with influential people. I did receive the *petit peu*; I should have been content but I was not. I aspired to something more than the stability offered by the economic system of the French État-providence. I was becoming utterly bored with the same repetitive tasks whose only purpose was to sustain me materially. Having satisfied the basic needs for food and shelter, the compendium of French bourgeois happiness, that *petit peu* soon was not enough. I wanted the infinite with an unprecedented intensity.

When I started venting my frustrations with my *petit bonheur*, to many I appeared to be just an ungrateful immigrant who received more than some citizens of France. They were right, I should have been grateful, done my job quietly, and followed the routine "métro, boulot, dodo" with humility and gratitude. Yet I was not capable of surrendering to its demands. I could not clearly see the reasons for this drive. It could be just an immigrant *mal de vivre* [existential unhappiness], but after all I had no nostalgia for Poland. The return was impossible even if the political situation changed in the future. I had enough distance from the Polish reality to be able to see that, despite my gloomy attitude, I had developed certain practical skills whose dormant presence I did not suspect when in Poland. I was able to learn tasks that I never envisioned before. I learned how to cook basic food, how to operate fax and copy machines, how to make binders, how to answer calls professionally, and I was even quite good at selling things to people that they did not really need. All banal but useful. In other words, France expanded my skills by forcing me to grow without my noticing it. Paris compelled me to become someone new; to have a new sense of *self*. The French language and lifestyle became my way of being. I started earning compliments: "you people from Eastern Europe, you are just like us, and this is why you assimilate so quickly."

I wish it was that simple! It wasn't. French and the people who had spoken it from birth had a different relationship to it. It was theirs, it was in their system, and it was their *body* language. In my case it was a choice, though encouraged by external circumstances. French was the idiom of the Other, and my relationship to it was like that of a lover to a beloved. I liked the idea of being immersed in it, speaking it, and using it at work. But like in the lovers' embrace when it relaxes its grip, one feels left to one's lonely fate again and again. French was external to me, even though I desired our oneness. This is possibly the nature of a good marriage that keeps two poles together despite periods of attraction and rejection. My relationship with French was meant to be like a marital commitment, though I did not know it yet, nor would I until the early 1980s.

The conjugal routine with French was to be disturbed by a romance-like vagary in Spain. After a year of service at the Etablissements Daloze, I earned my first paid five-week vacation. Through a Polish connection I was invited to spend three weeks near Alicante, a port city along the southern coast of Spain on the Mediterranean. A group of people rented a house in a village called Los Balcones that was, in fact, a summer colony of Polish World War II veterans from England. I took a train from Paris, and after some delay, I reached my final destination of Taragona, around midnight. I was concerned about getting there so late. To my surprise all of the town including the children were outdoors, taking advantage of evening's cool air. The warm air felt pleasant on my skin and I was surprised to have such a warm temperature at such a late hour. In the rudimentary Spanish that I had learned while still in Poland, I asked for directions. With the help of a group of people, they figured out what I was doing there and where I was heading. They called a taxi for me and dispatched it to Los Balcones.

Spain became the most dangerous rival for France, and for French, in my life. In an atavistic undercurrent I felt connected to it immediately. A year after the enchanting summer on the Costa Blanca, I spent my second five-week paid vacation in Salamanca doing a summer language course in Spanish. I learned Spanish very quickly at the language school of the Universidad Pontificia [Pontifical University of Salamanca]. I returned to Salamanca twenty years later to learned that the institution was built just before the suppression of the Jesuits in the eighteenth century, and that the main hall displayed the drawing representing the life of Ignatius of Loyola and the history of the Society of Jesus. But that summer, this did not mean anything. That which had meaning was the experience of watching, from the vantage point of the Tormes River, an incandescent sunset over the new cathedral of Salamanca. It brightened my whole being in a such way that I never returned to the misanthropy of my early Parisian adulthood.

Chapter Five

Saint Louis de Gonzague: Foreshadowing

Warmed by crepuscular beams of light radiating from the sun setting over the Cathedral of Salamanca, I returned to Paris immune to its indifference to so many human destinies cast onto its bosom in the quest for better lives, or simply, for freedom. I resumed my duties at the Etablissements Daloze with an attitude of surrender to the fate that surprisingly, after the transformative summer in Salamanca, became more tolerable. One day, a new customer came into the print shop with a series of orders for leaflets. She was involved in the "free school" movement in France, protesting against the so-called "Savary Bill," proposed during the presidency of François Mitterrand, that aimed to limit the state financing of private schools and integrate them into the public sector.[1] This movement organized massive demonstrations which contributed to the fall of the government of Pierre Mauroy in July 1984. The woman became our regular customer. Having learned that I was a Polish immigrant, she told me that her husband was a former political refugee from Hungary. He escaped after the defeat of the 1956 uprising against the Soviet domination of that country. We naturally sympathized with one another.

Her two sons were students at the Jesuit high school in the neighborhood. After we became more acquainted, she asked me if I wanted to move on to a more suitable employment. She offered to help me find a job at that Jesuit school where she was very active as a parent and known for her involvement in the *école libre* movement. The most common job opportunity at the school was that of a *surveillant*, or colloquially *pion*, similar to a discipline supervisor. And indeed, a few months after our discussion there was an opening at the Petit Collège of the Saint-Louis de Gonzague School, located on Louis David Street in the sixteenth *arrondissement*. The Grand Collège, the preparatory high school, was situated on Franklin Street, and was referred to simply as

Franklin, with the nasal sound at the end as in Rodin. I was hired to supervise three levels: grades nine through seven, counting backward in the conventional French way when speaking of private schools. The grades corresponded to the ages eight through ten years old. There were three sections of thirty students at each level, which amounted to approximately 270 pupils.

Of course, after my year in Versailles as a *garçon au pair*, I could claim to have some *teaching* experience; at least I knew how to interact with children. My command of French was clearly an advantage for which I was often complimented. My role appeared to be actually more important that I had anticipated. Discipline in French private schools was taken very seriously. Pupils were expected to form ranks in the courtyard after arriving at school in the morning, and the principal, Mademoiselle de Folin de la Fontaine and I were to salute their readiness for schoolwork. If some parents were late in bringing their child to school, they received a scornful glance from Mademoiselle de Folin. If tardiness was chronic, eventually the pupils would not be allowed in school at least for the first hour. Once the pupils entered their classrooms, Mademoiselle de Folin and I would meet. I received the orders for the day. At those meetings, Mademoiselle would often share with me, in a very frank French fashion, which teacher was difficult to manage, which parents were useful for the school despite their academically hopeless progeny, or whose son's behavior we had to endure because of the parent's political position. To illustrate the kind of pedigree we were dealing with, it is enough to say that a son of Nicolas Sarkozy attended the school just before his father became the president.

My next task was to prepare for recess during which I supervised the courtyard. In general, students would play in a relative peaceful manner. Occasionally, I had to arbitrate some dispute after hearing a report "he said a bad word," or "he is cheating at our game," or "he is lying." I was the absolute authority on the courtyard. To be called to mediate a controversy, it was enough for a pupil to scream, "Monsieur Motyka!" and I would intervene and pronounce a verdict. In rare instances, I would send someone to the office of Mademoiselle de Folin, which could result in a suspension or the notification of parents.

Mademoiselle de Folin was quite a personage. It was said that her genealogy went back to the family of the famous seventeenth-century fabulist Jean de la Fontaine. She must have been a very good classroom teacher, displayed often by her interaction with pupils. As the principal, her name had more impact than her actual administrative skills, which were limited to sending paper memos of little importance all day long for me to dispatch to the appropriate address. She favored younger teachers over the experienced ones, who often challenged her if her directives came across as confusing or questionable. The most difficult teacher was Mademoiselle de Linval, originally from the Antilles, who would be quite direct with the principal. It was not rare to hear about the encounters at our meetings, "Mademoiselle de Folin, look straight into my eyes, you are lying again." Then, the principal would play the role of a martyr, fallen pray to unruly employees entrusted to her supervision by the school board. The rest of the assembly, particularly the younger ones, seeking to preserve Mademoiselle de Folin's favors, would exchange with her a few compassionate glances.

The Jesuit presence in the Petit Collège was limited to two older priests: Père Desbains and Père Gille. They taught catechism, heard confessions, and presided over religious festivities organized by the school. Often, during the time between recesses, le père Gille, whose office was located next to mine, would knock on my door to chat about the life of the Petit Collège. The emotional outbursts of Mademoiselle de Linval toward Mademoiselle de Folin would be one of the favorite pretexts for our mutual analysis of the social context of the school.

Some debriefing would concern the new secretary that was sent from Franklin to work under Mademoiselle de Folin. The expectation was that Mademoiselle de Folin would find a reason to fire Madame Claudine Clavereul, whose work performance was inadequate, to say the least. As expected, she was on medical leave most of the time, and when she did come to work, she was usually late and looked for occasions to chat with me or some other employee. A divorcee of forty-something, who wore a tight short skirt and high heals, Claudine represented a moral danger in the eyes of Mademoiselle de Folin, who tended to impede any *tête-à-tête* between the new secretary and me by suddenly appearing in the hall. Le père Gille particularly enjoyed commenting on Claudine's habit of climbing into her office through the window. Being chronically late, she would circumvent the building's entrance by bending to her knees while passing under the window of Mademoiselle de Folin's office—not an easy task in her skirt and fashionable heels. The outfit was not helpful either in climbing through the window of her office, but with practice she became very agile. Mademoiselle de Folin eventually managed to dismiss her after daily documenting her unprofessional conduct and providing a financial settlement.

For almost three years, these characters populated my social landscape. The work, although not highly compensated, gave me that *petit peu* that I thought would end my aspirations for any further professional advancement in life. I had a tiny Parisian studio, a minimum wage, I supervised the children of people of notoriety or influence, and the colleagues with whom I worked with were kind to me, expressing appreciation for my contribution to the life of the school. Parents often expressed their curiosity about me as well as their gratitude for my care of their children. I could see that the environment created by the Catholic school mirrored the ties that one builds with one's own relatives. We lived like a family, sharing our lives in a communal intimacy, and very differently from the North American model—as I was to discover later. In America, newcomers from Europe are introduced to rules of conduct in the workplace with which they are expected to comply in order to stay employed. In France, the boundaries between the professional conduct and a more personal attitude and relationship are not clearly distinguishable. This often has an adversarial impact on the atmosphere. But the French unionized system tolerates that luxury of feeling at home in the work environment. There is a good and a bad side to this system, however. The business context does not really require a professional persona, therefore, makes it possible for one to interact with colleagues in a more authentic way. On the other hand, emotions involved in an authentic, natural human interaction might have a negative impact on productivity by creating diversions from the main purpose of coming to work.

Speaking of family, I was reaching the age at which the question about the future started burgeoning. The family of the Petit Collège was clearly not enough. What was the purpose of my life? Would I ever be able to do anything else in my life other than being "Monsieur Motyka," a man monitoring the school playground? I had a substantial amount of academic coursework but no real degree. I could not be advanced to the position of a classroom teacher even though I successfully substituted for teachers on short-term sick leave. All the classroom teachers had a degree in elementary education. I would not be able to pursue additional professional development without completing a degree. I sensed that the school would, in fact, like me to stay there forever at the same professional level.

One day, however, the second Jesuit priest, le père Desbains, with whom I had had little exchange, asked me if I had any plans for the future. I was surprised by the question knowing that Mademoiselle de Folin would not like that intrusion for fear that I might get the idea of seeking another position. But le père Desbains added plainly that I did not look like someone for whom the job as a *pion* was the final destination of his professional career. It was a liberating intervention that freed me from the rising guilt of being an incorrigible dreamer about something more than that *petit peu* that I eventually received through employment at Saint-Louis de Gonzague.

The dream was unleashed by an unexpected encounter with Americans in Paris and their culture. Infatuated with Frenchness as I had been in my youth, I had no interest in America except for the good movies of the 1970s and 1980s. I did not like the sound of the English language, and the whole culture was beyond the scope of my intellectual horizon. Nevertheless, being a Pole, I did not have in me the Western European anti-Americanism typical of my peers in France. My parents had instilled in me a sense of admiration for America. As a child, when watching or listening to Polish television or radio, my father would instruct me about not believing the official political propaganda but to read between the lines of what was officially communicated. I still hear the voice of the news presenter from the time of the Vietnam War, issuing the praise of "the heroic Vietnamese nation brutally invaded by the imperialist forces." Of course, my father saw in it the heroic attempt by the United States to stop the spread of the Soviet influence under the guise of international communism. Each evening he would compare the Polish version of the news with that of the Voice of America or the BBC commenting on the lies of the pro-Soviet propaganda. My mother was more sensitive to the tragic fate of the Vietnamese who suffered burning from napalm attacks and were trapped in the middle between the two imperialist giants.

I vividly remember watching the lunar landing with my parents and my father commenting, "look what the Americans can do, the Soviets will never land on the moon." And in fact they never did it. My mother always encouraged me to watch all of the Walt Disney movies shown on Polish television because they usually fostered perseverance in people and showed that the virtue of goodness always wins. Perhaps this unconscious acquisition of the virtue of perseverance started paying off after landing in Paris and being confronted with adulthood.

Nonetheless, perseverance was not exactly the chief personality characteristic of the Americans whom I met in Paris. It was a rather nonchalance that contrasted greatly with the French bourgeois cautiousness. The Americans who happened to live in Paris in the 1980s were unconcerned about issues such as universal healthcare, employment benefits, and retirement plans. They came to Paris in search of the *meaning of life* that was apparently not easy to find in their complicated multicultural landscape.

My first encounter with Americans was at an English language school in Le Marais, a small private business that employed recent graduates of US universities, who were seeking European adventures. I was convinced by a friend, Elżbieta Wewiórska, to learn English which she believed would broaden our chances for employment. The contact with the language opened the door to the culture that had the determining impact on my future. English appeared to be a much harder language than Spanish. Its unpredictable pronunciation rules unsettled my instinct for regularity that developed by the study of Romance languages. Contractions that English usage allows in educated speech came across as an irrecoverable shock. Idiomatic prepositional phrases that did not make any sense at first glance, for me, plagued my clarity of expression and hindered quick learning. Moreover, the use of articles seemed to be contrary to any rules in French despite the semblance of terms such as "definite" or "indefinite." Where French would require the indefinite or partitive article, English would not take anything. This endeavor promised to be a lifelong battle. Fortunately, my reading skills developed quickly because of many cognates between French and English—easier to recognize in a written discourse than in speaking due to major phonetic alterations.

More than language study, the school of English meant contact with the New World that had a completely different outlook on the world. Through our teacher Keith, we met a group of Americans whose experience as immigrants or residents of Paris were much different than ours. For the most part, they were new graduates from college who craved a foreign experience. They learned enough French to get by. Some, like Keith, had a good command of the language and pursued their studies at the university. They looked at us as if we were curious specimens formed by a repressive regime, and they expressed the wish to have been more repressed or confined in their own upbringing by more demanding social and political strictures. We would assure them that there was no reason to be envious.

Soon Elżbieta and I realized that the school was a *rip-off* for students as well as for teachers. We left the school in Le Marais after a few months and enrolled in courses offered at the American Church on Quai d'Orsay. But, we cultivated our relationship with Americans whom we had met through our first school. Keith, our main instructor, had a gift for bringing people together in a Californian way, sometimes unaware of potential tensions that new encounters might raise. For the most part, the social network he helped create in that pre-Facebook reality was fortunate. People enjoyed each other's company, and we, economic immigrants, benefited greatly from the perspective that the Americans shed on Paris. They were interested in art and music, which they knew and appreciated much more than Europeans usually want to give Americans credit. Visits to museums, outings to concerts, and discussions on culture and literature filled our free time.

The most transforming influence was the American challenge to the French bourgeois longing for that *petit peu* that I felt compelled to embrace. Instead of talking about the minimum wage, work benefits, and retirement plans, we were talking about Fyodor Dostoyevsky, Stendhal, Albert Camus, Simone Weil, Czeslaw Milosz, and, of course, Ernest Hemingway. And, it was at that time that I discovered jazz and Gospel music. I realized why jazz had been so popular in communist Poland. It carried with it the breath of freedom that the political power was not able to suppress. It triggered the awakening of the soul, and initiated in the body, movement that music dictated. For me, a new Parisian, it kindled enthusiasm for shedding the bourgeois ideal of the *petit peu* and "gave me wings to fly."

My initiation to Gospel music happened in the Théâtre du Châtelet where an American group performed on a concert tour. Unlike jazz, Gospel music presented some initial resistance, particularly because of a sequence of healing by the "laying on of hands," a ritual that was carried out by some of the singers for those who wanted to surrender to their spiritual powers. I was clearly too Catholic for that. But my American friend, who suggested the concert, went on to be touched by the healers. As she, a Jew from New York, explained it to me, she grew up in a segregated neighborhood marked by fear of African Americans. Her high school experience of unsuccessful racial integration left some deep scars that she longed to cure. And, indeed, she believed that Paris offered her a chance to make a first step toward overcoming the uneasiness that had been instilled in her since her teenage years. Notwithstanding my resistance to the healing ritual, the singing that emanated from the heart of the performers touched me deeply. It was a naked praise of God's greatness, unfiltered by the secularizing fashions of the European West. It resonated with the same power for me as it did some ten years later when I was discerning my religious vocation as a parishioner of Saint Patrick's Church, a Roman Catholic church serving a predominantly African American congregation in West Oakland, California.

American culture brought about a real danger to my frame of mind that considered French culture as the apogee of human artistic creativity and intellectual thought. The Americans of Paris subverted the firmness of that conviction. If the mastery of English had not been such a challenge, French might have lost its place at that time. Yet it did not because my English was to remain broken for many years ahead, and my American friends insisted in fact that we communicate in French so that they could increase their own proficiency. In that context, reading was my main source of satisfaction. I eventually read my first novel entirely in English—Hemingway's *The Sun Also Rises*.[2]

Reaching the point of reading the book entirely in English provided me with great pleasure. Additional pleasure arose from the novel's characters; I was identifying with their desire to escape from Paris to Spain, the Spain that enlightened in me feelings corresponding to those of the novel's protagonists. The title itself pointed to the Sun whose setting had left me with an unforgettable impression of the infinite. Moreover, the characters lived with many complex psychological problems that, I suspected, could be detected among our American companions. There was some instability in their relationships; there was ease in dissolving a relationship when one person became a burden to another's pursuit of fulfillment. This attitude was very different from my attempt to cultivate fidelity in my human relationships. I surrounded my few friendships with a shrine that required committed attendance and care. Fidelity in friendship has remained one of the characteristics that I recognize in my personality, to the extent that it might become burdensome for those who have fewer scruples about severing affective ties that are no longer convenient at a given moment of their lives.

From a distance, now, I suspect that our American friends in Paris sensed that these incompatibilities were soon to arise, and when there was a retrospective of the 1977 Wim Wenders film, *The American Friend*, I was invited to see the movie. The dark depiction of the relationship between the protagonists, portraying them as incapable of establishing lasting closeness, was meant as a warning.[3] It was to signify: "we are here to have fun, to grow intellectually, but we will leave in the near future to pursue our dream of independence which we not only drink with our mother's milk but also reinforce by the national ideal of freedom propagated by our democratic constitution." I ignored the warning at that time and deepened my *affair* with America to the extent that English has eventually become my main language of expression in which I compose this account.

The culminating point of my American fascination was the encounter with Jane Dickenson who came to Paris, as most Americans did, to discover the quintessential Europe whose culture she admired and extensively studied. Jane was committed to the ideas of the philosophers she admired, to the point that she lived through their ideas and did not leave any room for the profanity of cheap entertainment or other distractions. Kierkegaard, Nietzsche, and Simone Weil populated her imagination and established a magisterium of thought that left little room for the excesses of popular culture. My exchange with Jane brought me to a different level intellectually and humanly. She taught me how to discard or ignore anything that inhibited my trajectory toward genuine intellectual growth. Our interaction challenged my tendency to intellectual idleness because of her scornful view of television and entertainment in general. In my limited free time, I started rereading Dostoevsky and opened *La Pesanteur et la grâce*, by Weil, which Jane offered to me.[4] Weil's collection of short philosophical reflections looks to rehabilitate the fragile side of our human experience: the tragic element in our humanity makes up the best of who we potentially may become. It plunges us into a perpetual attempt to rise above the overpowering weight of the forces of gravity that restrain us as we strive to reach the realm of lightness where forces of depression have no more power over us. Reading Simone Weil was a prelude, as I can tell now, to the spiritual exercises of Ignatius of Loyola that call for self-emptying in order to reach the realm of the *self*, receptive to being *lifted by grace*. And as in the spiritual retreat, initial forces of gravity form a block that obstructs the flow of spiritual energy, *La Pesanteur et la grâce* generated resistance in me. I barely recognized that it was the bourgeois *petit peu* that allowed me to live more or less like the Parisian masses did, and here I met someone who started exercising a subversive influence that triggered insubordination to what seemed like the emergence of stability.

The encounter with Americans and their culture disturbed the constitution of a new *self* in me that was inclined to compromise with the status quo and to accept the limitations that I perceived Paris had forced on me. Jane, in a very bold way, helped to revive the impulses that had a Platonic sweep in their power to fly beyond the confines of bourgeois gravity.

Yet it would be mistaken to give the impression that Jane was an austere adept of her intellectual masters only. She was too beautiful to be exclusively a philosopher. She liked good wine, authentic ethnic food, and all kinds of pop music. She was a committed jogger and not a particularly early riser.

Aware of those trivial aspects of Jane's humanity, which belonged to the realm of gravity rather than to the one of grace, I decided to embark on the next stage of my journey. It was to be in America.

When I announced to Mademoiselle de Folin that I intended to leave the school and move to the United States, she was distressed. She ordered silence about it until the time came to announce it. She feared that the community might attribute my departure to her difficult personality. For a few months it was a *secret de polichinelle*, an open secret. Le père Desbains commented, "Didn't I tell you this was a temporary shelter for you?" The day of goodbyes came; students offered me a large card with thank you notes and shook my hand. Only at the time of that farewell, did I realize that that stage of my life was actually meaningful to others. Until then, I had had a deprecating sense of having a job that was not well paid and that the French in general did not want to do. Noticing glimpses of emotion in students as well as my colleagues' reactions to my departure made me grasp the scope of my influence on people's life. It was in fact more than just a job. There was an element of mission and of service in it. Retrospectively, I believe that the seed of a future religious vocation was *watered* during my experience of working at the Petit Collège, where the Jesuit spirit remained well alive despite a scarce presence of Jesuits themselves.

Chapter Six

San Francisco

New World, New Life

I landed in San Francisco at night on April 1, 1989. It was not a joke. I was brought to a home in the Oakland Hills. The next day I visited the city of Oakland in the area of Lake Merritt. Surprisingly, it was a misty day, and very different from the *cliché* image of California. But the smell of the luxuriant vegetation fulfilled the expectation of being in a promised land. It enveloped my senses with the enchantment that was telling, that even if I were to become a street bum, which I swore never to do in my visa application, I would actually find it more satisfying than living in a Parisian studio. The world opened its gates to me a big way. After seeing the campus of the University of California, Berkeley, a dream revisited me, and that was to enroll and obtain a degree in the United States.

As I started settling in the new cultural reality, I soon found that, unlike in Europe there were opportunities for me regarding education. I had my academic records evaluated and was advised that it would take me at least two years to earn a bachelor's degree. The equivalency system was stinging. However, San Francisco State University was willing to accept me for the next year if I applied formally in the fall. I did so and had a year to wait. The year passed by quickly. With my work experience in Paris, I found a clerical summer job in the office of the McGraw-Hill publishing house in Berkeley, using my expertise for making photocopies. Soon, a Czech woman, Marcela, a graphic designer for the company, initiated me into rudiments of composition. Given the closeness of Czech to Polish language, She explained the job to me in Czech which I understood better at the time, than I did English. We shared our emotions at the unraveling of the Communist block by an amazing series of peaceful revolutions. It was also the year of the Tiananmen

Square protests that ended in the massacre of hundreds of students and civilians on June 4, 1989. Without Marcela's company, I would have barely noticed anything outside my private revolution that required a great deal of effort to make ends meet financially.

After the summer job at McGraw-Hill, I was able to find another position, based on my prior educational experience at Petit Collège of the Saint-Louis de Gonzague. I became a teacher for an after school program called Enrichment Plus. Like my job in Paris, this was another job that the local educators did not want, but was perfect for me. I had to organize some games, including baseball whose rules I do not understand until this day! I was good at leading drawing and painting activities, and I offered a French class. In exchange, I was learning English from the children. Given the school's location in a wealthy neighborhood of Oakland, a considerable number of staff members and pupils were middle- and upper-middle class African Americans. I deepened my understanding of the new culture that I first encountered through the Gospel concert in the Théâtre of Châtelet. African American women knew how to enforce discipline more effectively than Mademoiselle de Folin herself. Vera, the head teacher, would only say "time out" in case of unruly conduct, and the kid would obey without questioning. Despite the *in progress* state of my English language skills, the African American colleagues and students accepted me as one of their own because I was a clear outsider to the contentious history of the relationships between the whites and the blacks in this country. My otherness did not carry in its presence a trigger of resentment. As I later discovered, being of Polish origin was not always an advantage in white, middle-class American circles, yet among the African Americans in California, it was not an obstacle for developing friendly ties.

Little by little, diverse strains of my new existence started falling in place and merged toward a clearer destiny. I was accepted by San Francisco State University and waited, with a dose of anguish, for the prospect of resuming my studies and earning my first university degree. I resigned from my after-school Enrichment Plus position and began university. I was also able to find clerical work in the Department of Foreign Languages. The secretary, Anne Hoedt, bilingual in French and English, was delighted to have me in the office and requested that we speak only French. Moreover, her assistant, Claire Abramovitz, was French. Thus began my return to French, despite my desire to work in an English-speaking environment in order to perfect the language.

The two years at San Francisco State represent probably the most exciting period in my life. The realistic objective of earning a degree energized me considerably. I calculated how I needed to accomplish the academic requirements within two years to graduate. I often needed to enroll in five courses per semester. Most of the courses required were needed to satisfy the general education requirements that the European system did not have. However, most of my coursework from Poland and France had been accepted toward a major in French for which I needed to complete only the residency requirements. I loved all my courses with the exception of statistics, and not because the class was poor, but simply because it showed that my talent did not lie in quantitative science. Classes in English, philosophy, religious studies, and human biology were true delights. I learned rhetorical devices of English composition very quickly, and, oh miracle!, the teachers did not comment on my ideas as "contestable." On the contrary, if they were "contestable," it meant that there was a genuine value resulting from personal input. I loved, in particular, the humanities course taught by Professor Sandra Luft whose exceptional pedagogical approach strengthened my interest in philosophical readings. The course's title was "Humanism and Mysticism" and included readings from Plato, Pico della Mirandolla, Meister Eckhart, Sartre, Boccaccio, and Suzuki. Professor Luft lectured but always as a response to our questions or issues that our papers raised. The teaching performance was so different from the resigned attitude of the philosophy instructors in Poland who assumed that our generation, victim of the communist brainwash, was a generation lost, or incapable, of any genuine philosophical thought or discourse.

Of great personal value was the Human Biology course which stimulated my curiosity about the work, or processes, of the human machine: our body. The instructor, with whom I later took a bioethics class, was clearly a believer. I could detect his convictions through a pronounced fascination with the orderliness of our organism. For him, it was obvious that the forces of chaos alone could not produce life and arrange it in such a harmonious system. These core requirements revived the seed of vocation in me to pursue infinity. Through the pleasure of learning in engaging courses, my desire to progress beyond the *petit peu* was nourished. Ultimately the basic knowledge of human physiology was useful for my diverse experiments during my Jesuit formation: in a hospital, in a detention center, or at a parish.

After the Sorbonne experience, French literature classes at San Francisco State University appeared to be the reversal of that passive absorption of conventional wisdom that allowed only one *incontestable* interpretation, that of course, must agree with that of the teacher. I remember, particularly fondly, classes I took with Professor Elizabeth Wright, who helped me view and interpret the richness of French literature in a new light. Given my proficiency in French and credit for substantial coursework, I was allowed to enroll in graduate courses while completing my bachelors program. Professor Wright taught subjects in medieval and early modern literature. Suddenly, a subject matter, that I had vowed to abandon after dulling *explications de texte* in the *travaux dirigés* [discussion sections] of the Sorbonne, beckoned to me with an unsuspected appeal. Moreover, medieval and renaissance poetry and prose seemed suddenly relevant and exotic in this land of swiftly changing cultural trends.

Notwithstanding this intellectual awakening, some residual resistance emerged in the case of fulfilling the requirement of modern French literature. I chose a course on modern poetry. Although the course was well organized in a French manner and adapted to the needs of American students, the classroom presence of the professor naturally evoked the experience of the French university and affected my attitude toward the subject. Despite the quality of the teaching, it awakened the dormant bitterness like a flash. I did well in the course because of my superior command of French but had to control my temper throughout the class; I did not want to jeopardize my return to academia.

Another challenge for me in my US college experience was my poor typing. Despite having taken a class at a community college, I have never mastered the art of typing to a satisfactory level. Contrary to Europe, here written papers were the essential part of more advanced academic work and had to be typed. At this time, computers only began to be widely used. Fortunately, Claire and other colleagues in the office of Foreign Languages helped type my papers and could do it in the blink of an eye.

In the French graduate courses I met master's students, among whom was Michèle Simon. Michèle and I became instantaneous friends. We met on Bay Area Rapid Transit, the train/subway system in San Francisco, otherwise known as BART. We were both on our way to the university and forgot to change trains at MacArthur station. While waiting for the next train, I initiated a conversation. I knew who Michèle was because she worked as a teaching assistant for French language courses and picked up her mail in the office. We started our conversation in English, which, although fluent and grammatically impeccable, sounded just like French, therefore, we soon switched to French. Michèle and I shared our disenchantment with the French educational system and enthusiasm for American higher education. She was a *Pied Noir* of French and Italian descent, born in Algeria, then repatriated to France in her early teens. She arrived in the United States in her mid-twenties motivated by her fascinations with the Beatniks. Jack Kerouac being her hero, she settled in the Bay Area that became her home. After our fortuitous meeting on the way to San Francisco State University, for the subsequent fifteen years, we interacted exclusively in French unless a third party who did not speak French was involved in the conversation.

The friendship with Michèle restored French to its centrality in my affective life; it filled the gaps left by my limited communicative competence in English. In a near fatalistic pursuit, French reclaimed its right to intimacy in communication. My interest in pursuing an education rather than quick money, as well as my past in France, set me apart immediately from the Polish community. Therefore, on this side of the Atlantic, I did not have many opportunities to speak in Polish. I did not have the desire to bond with the members of the local Polish community given the disparity of our interests. As the applied linguist Stephen Krashen, the father of the natural approach in second language education, would confirm, I had enough time in France for the acquisition of French to happen. According to Krashen's estimate, a complete acquisition of a second language, that is, absorption of a second idiom, occurs naturally within six years of full exposure to the context in which that language is used. Krashen contrasts acquisition with the process of learning that involves a conscious effort to master the foreign idiom, often in a short period.[1] Therefore, in my new linguistic situation, French had been made ready to take the place Polish had occupied in France in its relation to French, a private code averting the censorship of the mainstream culture. There was one crucial difference though: while knowing French would eventually provide for my living given its social status in California, conversely, Polish had no practical application.

The rise of the French language in its importance in my life coincided with a loosening of ties with the American cohort I had met in Paris, and who, for the most part, had settled in California. After I was accepted by San Francisco State University, Jane was admitted to a doctoral program at one of the most prestigious universities in the United States, unfortunately located on the other side of the country. It was either *naïveté* on my part, or perhaps, God's jealous irruption into my life that placed me at this crossroad and caused our interests to bifurcate. I was too excited by my return to school to give up this new chance in my life, and feeling my own attachment to the idea, I also did not want to divert Jane from pursuing the same path that I wanted to follow. Our decisions were detrimental in their impact on our plans. Yet the sacrifice of close friendship for a higher goal, created for both of us unexpected fulfillment.

As my American friendships were giving in to the pressures of a career and intellectual growth, the tormenting specter of the American friend induced by Wim Wenders's film, *The American Friend*, returned to haunt me, causing doubts about the prospects of spending the rest of my life in this country.[2] I had overcome the desire of settling for that bourgeois *petit peu*. The educational opportunities of America had removed my concerns for a retirement pension and a small *chez moi*. My new opportunities also opened a new horizon for an uncharted adventure beyond the conventional wisdom of the European middle class. Nevertheless, on an affective level, it was very difficult for me to relinquish the human *petit peu* that would come from the warmth of close human relationships. I cherished the illusion of having my private bourgeois joys of hearth and home.

In this period of new social reconfiguration, consolation came from Professor Wright's course on medieval poetry. We studied the texts in modern French translation. The twelfth-century convention of courtly love captivated my imagination. Again, French literature exercised the same power to transport me to the realm of an ideal and dream as it had done in communist Poland. The poetry of the Provençal poet Joffré Rudel corresponded quite precisely to my state of mind. He coined the concept of "distant love" which he celebrates in one of his best-known poems, "Lanquan li jorn son lonc en mai":

> Lanquan li jorn son lonc en mai
> m'es belhs dous chans d'auzelhs de lonh,
> e quan me sui partitz de lai
> remembra.m d'un' amor de lonh;[3]

> [When the days are long in May,
> I like a sweet song of the birds from afar,
> and when I have gone away from there
> They bring to mind a love from afar.][4]

Jaufré's delectation of "distant love" was certainly ambivalent. The state of longing was as important as the object of his desire. Commentators speculate about who the distant lady was. His *vida,* a short biography that accompanied the early manuscript collections of the Troubadours' poems, speaks of his love for the Princess of Tripoli in whose arms he ended his life after undertaking an exhausting sea journey to find her.

By all means there was something appealing in that "distant love," a deferred desire that stirred the waves of imagination in search of a substitute for an absence impossible to fill. Jaufré's poetry conveyed to me the value of fidelity and consistency as an existential generative principle. Having been disappointed in human commerce, I began to cultivate longing for the sake of longing itself. I could find appeasement only in arduous study and work. Plato's *Phaedrus*, Meister Eckhart's selected writings, and Giovanni Pico della Mirandola's *Oration on the Dignity of Man*, read in Professor Luft's class helped me accept my new condition of a man who needed to stand on his own two feet, detached from the social network that supplied me with a temporary identity.[5] By chance I heard Elvis's song "Lonesome Cowboy" and thought, "Ah, now, after a few years in America, I understand why someone would come up with lyrics of that sort." The expanse of the horizon pointing to an unconquered wilderness creates in the people here a sense of independence, which is very different from the communal ways of the European civilization. So, humming with Presley, I let my fancy fly,

> Will I ever leave this lonesome valley
> Really see the lights that shine
> Gotta find what lies beyond the mountain
> Gotta rope and tie that dream of mine.[6]

It became apparent to me that my dream had to be roped and tied. Like the charioteer in Plato's *Phaedrus*, I had to harness the driving forces in me and direct them toward a destination able to soothe the restlessness in me that desired to achieve a state where longing was no more.

As I was giving in to the gloom of lonesomeness, reminiscent of my Parisian misanthropic phase, Professor Wright's course on Renaissance prose came across as a happy diversion. We read *Gargantua* and *Pantagruel* by Fraçois Rabelais. The preposterous adventures of the giants Gargantua and his son Pantagruel provided comic relief to my preoccupation with the future.[7] Reading primary texts from the Renaissance, at the graduate level, unveiled an unexpected facet of the period. While the communist propaganda in Poland represented the Renaissance as the reversal of medieval obscurantism and as the end of irrationalism and religious bigotry, Rabelais's books do not support those claims by any obvious means. In truth, the divine never ceased to be the ultimate reference in the Renaissance. For example, Rabelais's protagonists encounter various human types whereby they underscore the irony of human attempts to solve the mysteries of human existence. Rabelais physician delights in the hyperbolic depiction of the scabrous aspects of human reality through which he conveys lessons in humility and derides pitilessly the vanity of those who think they can avert the common human destiny of clumsy creatures. Our humanity has much in common with the animal world even though many aspire to ascend to the level of angelic beings. Healthy laughter, induced by Rabelais's humor, deflated the mood of self-pity I was in danger of yielding to.

Whereas Rabelais's fabulous imagination was a draw for readers, another representative author of the period, Michel de Montaigne gained notoriety by focusing his writing on his own experience. To a considerable extent, this introspective approach remains in the background of my own literary enterprise. He famously states in the prologue of the *Essays* (Au Lecteur [To the Reader], "Ainsi, lecteur, je suis moy-mesmes la matiere de mon livre; ce n'est pas la raison que tu employes ton loisir en un subject si frivole et si vain" ["And therefore, Reader, I myself am the subject of my book: it is not reasonable that you should employ your leisure on a topic so frivolous and so vain."][8] Some ambiguity hides behind these words: does he really think his project is frivolous because of its self-centeredness? Maybe it is simply a rhetorical twist that works as a publicity device for piquing the curiosity of whoever might open the first page. Whatever the dominant intention of this writing project might really be, its power lies in its bold affirmation of the individuals' right to position themselves *vis-à-vis* history they cannot control. He concludes his essay "On freedom of conscience" by the following statement, "Yet for the honour and piety of our kings I prefer to believe that, since they could not do what they wished, they pretended to wish to do what they could."[9] A great principle of adaptation to the circumstances that frees us from the guilt of not having done what we possibly could not, provided we did freely that which was in our power and which we believed to be right and necessary. One must remember that Montaigne wrote his *Essays* in the tumultuous era of the French wars of religion between the Catholics and the French Protestants, the Huguenots. War inculcated in him a profound sense of pessimism and disenchantment with humanity. He retired in his *château* near Bordeaux and decided to share his wisdom on paper, not for didactic purposes but as an exploration of the self. Montaigne's readings appeased my sense of inadequacy and encouraged me to inhabit lonesomeness as a genuine virtue rather than a bitter withdrawal from human commerce. To enjoy my new freedom, I needed greater detachment from all that I still desired, or the human *petit peu* that life seemed to be taking away from me.

Another encounter of crucial importance for my future was in an undergraduate course on eighteenth-century French literature. The course was offered by Professor Martin, a popular instructor in his early sixties, whose striking story-telling quality illustrated the meaning of the texts and connected them to contemporary culture. He had an extensive background in philosophy and sociology, and, therefore, literature of the French Enlightenment *philosophes* made a good fit. One of the readings he included in the course was *Les Bijoux indiscrets*, by Denis Diderot, a novel published anonymously in 1748. In the story, the sultan Mangogul of the Congo disposes of a magic ring that makes women's genitals ("jewels") talk. Diderot aims to expose secrets of women's feelings and thoughts about desire and sexuality to the general public, that without this clever stratagem would remain a social taboo.[10] I found this libertine novel quite repetitive and dull with its sensationalist and exhibitionist rendering of adulterous affairs at the sultan's court, but Professor Martin clearly liked the book. Sensing that, I wrote my paper for the course on that topic—something rather conventional, with a focus on sexual repression and the need for honesty in sexual matters without which we build a hypocritical society imposing undue limitations on individual freedom. The instructor responded positively to my paper to the extent that he thought it was publishable. It was not really; it lacked scholarly rigor but contained some fresh ideas and likely pointed to some affinities between Professor Martin and myself. I surmised that Professor Martin sensed that my un-Californian restraint was a result of a repressive upbringing that, he might have suspected, had its source in Catholicism (as in his case, of which I was about to hear). How could he understand that I owed my restraint and lack of trust not to Catholicism, but rather to the Polish version of socialism? Most importantly, however, the paper contributed to redirecting my future from my intention of becoming a high school teacher to the pursuit of graduate education.

The flattering response of Professor Martin to my paper intrigued me and I wanted to learn more about who he was. My main source of information was Anne Hoedt and later Professor Martin himself. He was clearly francophone, although his English was as good as his French. He was not a Quebecois, which everybody assumed he was when hearing his slightly different intonation from that of the people from the metropolis. In reality, to my surprise, he was born and raised in a French-speaking village in New Hampshire. The account of his childhood pointed to a great deal of austerity in his very Catholic upbringing, marked by some extreme ascetic practices involving icy showers in undergarments, even in private, for fear of nudity. That explained to me why *Les Bijoux indiscrets* would have such an appeal for him, as a repudiation of all the inhibitions inculcated in his youth. But that was not all to the mystery of the man. One day, when Anne Hoedt experienced a personal crisis, she did not come to work and called the office asking for Professor Martin. When she returned to the office the next day, she disclosed to me that Professor Martin was a former priest who had left the priesthood, served in the US Army, and eventually became professor of French at San Francisco State University. In difficult moments Anne sought his pastoral qualities that laicization had not diminished in him.

It was these pastoral qualities that contributed to my decision to apply to graduate school. One day in the office, Professor Martin asked me what my plans were for the future. I replied that after graduation I was planning to join the "Teach for America" program, while working, to prepare for teaching certification. But he said that he saw me in a graduate school, and that he and his colleagues would write letters of recommendations on my behalf. This conversation changed the course of my life. I suddenly and unexpectedly pictured myself as a graduate student, possibly at UC Berkeley. Yet, I did not want to just study French. The rather forceful experience in the course with the French-trained instructor, evoking the bad experience at the Sorbonne, deterred me from committing several years to a possibly similar teaching style. After perusing university catalogues, I did learn that the program in Romance Languages and Literatures at UC Berkeley required proficiency in three major Romance languages: Spanish, French, and Italian. Applicants were to declare their major language, as well as their first and second collateral. My Spanish was already quite good; I had managed to include in my schedule advanced courses in composition, reading, and conversation. The second course was particularly beneficial, taught by an instructor from Spain, Professor Maribel Bremerman, with whom I sympathized immediately, and who happened to have her PhD from UC Berkeley. She also encouraged my graduate application to UC Berkeley. As for Italian, I realized, knowing Spanish I could read at the advanced level. Having studied it for a brief period in Poland, I remembered the rules of pronunciation, which were not difficult for a speaker of Polish with nearly an identical vowel quality system and similar fricative consonants. I decided that if I were accepted to the program, I would spend my summer studying Italian on my own. I applied declaring French as my major field, Spanish as the first collateral, and Italian as the second, but I had the secret intention to make Spanish my major field eventually, once admitted to the program.

Professor Bremerman embodied the memories from my trips and summer language studies in Spain. She had a delightful sense of humor, and despite being nearly retirement age, she wore very bright clothes and always a flower in her hair, a red or white carnation. When she entered the office, seeing me at the reception desk, she would give me a sign to remain silent and walked to empty her mailbox on tiptoes (in her pink heels), so as not to alert Anne Hoedt of her visit. Professor Bremerman (like many other instructors) would rather elude encounters with Anne in order not to be retained in a conversation, or more precisely in a monologue about the department. For her class, I read *One Hundred Years of Solitude*, by Gabriel García Márquez, the Colombian Nobel Prize recipient in literature, and a master of magic realism that was an enchantment in itself, punctuated by students' outbursts of laughter when the instructor provided a comment on the character's outlandish behavior.[11] Absorbing García Márquez's work in Spanish made me ready for graduate studies in that language.

Thus here I was, a multilingual subject, enjoying a formidable sense of freedom that the potentiality of passing from one linguistic territory to another offers. English had given me the freedom from French that confined me to the model of bourgeois happiness with the "little something" with which one was meant to be satisfied. But French had left an indelible imprint that would not erase that essential experience of becoming an adult in a free country. My life in English had unleashed, however, a dream about the possibility of success. It was an American dream that sneaks into the heart of whoever enters in contact with this energetic culture of enthusiasm and of easy human relations. Nevertheless, as one of the masters of the old continent had it, the Spanish playwright of the seventeenth-century Golden Age, Calderón de la Barca, dreams are only dreams ("sueños sueños son"[12]). One morning, one awakens, confronted with the reality and can remember but the sweetness of the dissipated fancy. Human relationships in the land of all promises, America, are subject to the law of dreaming and mutate like dreams themselves in pursuit of a new fanciful project.

The return to French embodied the old principle of fidelity, and an inner, half-conscious voice whispered: "Parisian streets formed you, you may like it or not but you may not shed the marks you have received on your heart." Spanish could free me from both, French and English, by opening a gate to the realm where the restricted *petit peu* made no sense nor did the climbing of the social ladder seem to matter at all. I was likely idealizing the Spanish-speaking reality because of my summer trips to Spain, trips that challenged the layer of my guarded *self*. I kept hearing echoes of the flamenco chant that

I had heard at a concert in Cadiz, with its naked authenticity of a passion without the makeup of bourgeois or capitalist politeness and restraint.

But I did not have the strength to say no to the dream of being a graduate student by moving to Spain, abandoning French, and starting a fresh domain of learning. After all, French had given direction to my life. I followed the protocol required for admission and applied to the graduate program. I prepared an essay in which I praised my dubious qualities of having an unusual life experience, asked for letters of recommendation, took the GRE test with poor results,... and, yes, the dream came true. In February of 1993 I received the notice from the Graduate Division of the University of California that I had been accepted to the program of Romance Languages and Literatures, commonly referred to as RLL. Moreover, to my great joy, I saw that the program was housed in the Department of Spanish and Portuguese, which reinforced my intention to opt, eventually, for Spanish as my first field. At the conclusion of that academic year I graduated from San Francisco State University with a Bachelor of Art in French.

Chapter Seven

O Beautiful!

The first phase of my graduate school experience could be seen as a diversion into the world of academic pride by succumbing to enticements of an ambitious academic career. For a time, I complacently gave in to the temptation of climbing the ladder leading to the heights of academic glory, of course, after fulfilling all the requirements ahead of me. The challenges of the climb consisted of pleasing everybody in order to receive positive letters of recommendations as well as securing introductions to important people in the field. I entered the illusion of grandeur that UC Berkeley has created and cultivates very successfully. I suppose I was not a bad student, but I could not jump into torrents of ambition which the university expected one to undertake. The university fostered in me a *manie de grandeur,* a delusional state so different from the *petit peu* bourgeois I was expected to embrace in France. This time, the call was to surpass the limitations of the *self* in a quasi Platonic transport somewhere above the rainbow to a "pays de Cocagne," a land of plenty which Charles Baudelaire depicts so seductively in his prose poem "L'Invitation au voyage":

> Un vrai pays de Cocagne, où tout est beau, riche, tranquille, honnête; où le luxe a plaisir à se mirer dans l'ordre; où la vie est grasse et douce à respirer; d'où le désordre, la turbulence et l'imprévu sont exclus; où le bonheur est marié au silence; où la cuisine elle-même est poétique, grasse et excitante à la fois; où tout vous ressemble, mon cher ange.[1]

> [A true land of Cockaigne, where all is beautiful, rich, tranquil, and honest; where luxury is pleased to mirror itself in order; where life is opulent, and sweet to breathe; from whence disorder, turbulence, and the unforeseen are excluded; where happiness is married to silence; where even the food is poetic, rich and exciting at the same time; where all things, my beloved, are like you.][2]

On a daily basis, the route to the land of Cockaigne was paved with trials in the form of term papers, qualifying exams, and the lengthy process of drafting my dissertation. Cockaigne was the reward for all the hardship of playing the game of ambition and pride. I followed the path leading to fame until something unexpected happened to me. When plunged into the intense labor on my dissertation, I heard the voices of the authors whom I had elected to study. They whispered to me, "we learned our distance to reality from our schooling in Jesuit institutions. This life is a clumsy approximation of something that lies above all the vain strife of modern academia."

But before I understood the sense of the old masters' call, I needed to experience, firsthand, the emptiness to which the academic routine led me. It took about three and a half years before the privileged, yet very difficult, time came to write my dissertation. This was a time of flirting with delusion, marked by attempts to rupture my intimate ties with French by switching to Spanish and Italian, and then eventually projecting myself as a type of *big shot* in a well-defined academic field. The city of Berkeley was a promise of the final destination in the "pays de Cocagne."

My period at UC Berkeley clearly represents the happiest secular period of my life. Real coffee in mushrooming *cafés à la française*, Cheeseboard, with its selection of cheeses and breads, and of course Chez Panisse, a French-inspired gourmet restaurant serving high quality meals, that is, with organic produce and carefully sourced ingredients. Even though I went there only once, invited after the completion of my first teaching semester by a grateful student of Serb origin, I was aware of this French enclave in Berkeley since coming to the city. Its existence stirred up nostalgic imaginary journeys to the South of France. Another landmark and symbol of *the good life* was the notorious Berkeley Bowl supermarket, with its fantastic display of fruits and vegetables from all around the world, though mostly grown locally and often organically, and sold at lower prices than in other comparable chain markets.

Yet coffee, cheese, and produce markets were not the only Euro-like attractions in this extraordinary university town. There was high culture. The Pacific Film Archive (PFA) became the major hangout for Michèle Simon and me. It was located in a wing of the university art museum building on Bancroft Avenue. PFA represented the strongest cultural link with Europe; the repertoire transported me in my imagination to the Accattone Cinema in the Latin Quarter of Paris. One could see Italian, French, and German classics as well as films from Eastern Europe. There, I saw the *Saragossa Manuscript* and met with the director, Wojciech Has, who came to present the restored version of the film.[3] His interpreter from Polish to English was the son of poet Czeslaw Milosz.

Besides enjoying the film offerings, Michèle introduced me to small amateur theater troupes, whose actors had professional ambition. They staged a variety of plays at different locations throughout the city. A frequent venue was the basement of La Val's Restaurant, on Euclid Avenue, where we followed the emergence of the troupes, such as, the Subterranean Shakespeare Theatre, or now, the professionalized Shotgun Players. It has been a thrill to observe for twenty years, the professional growth of its founder Patrick Dooley whose good looks at that time were reminiscent of Jude Law's, in Michèle's opinion. Conversing with Michèle in French was a life line for my bond with French that could have diminished while I was taking classes in Spanish and Italian literature.

It was a kind of *dolce vita*. Reading for courses, preparing my own curriculum, and enjoying the social and cultural atmosphere that Berkeley had to offer. I was somewhat careful with forming new relationships and remained fairly distant from my fellow graduate students. Recently, Tania Liberati, who entered the same program in Romance Languages and Literatures (RLL) some years after me, disclosed to me that I had the reputation of being a multilingual Polish aristocrat. I found it rather pleasant to have such a literary stereotype attributed to me rather than any of the common stereotypes attributed to some Poles in the United States.

The only student colleague with whom I socialized closely was Cornelia Peterson. She grew up in Berkeley but did not represent a stereotypical Berkeleyan type. She did not wear tie-dye nor was she particularly excited by all the organic naturals that Berkeley offers. In that sense, I myself went more *native* than she, a real native. Cornelia's father was a professor of engineering at UC Berkeley, her mother was a type of *grande dame*, with strong social skills that compensated for her husband's reserved personality. Cornelia inherited her mother's social skills, even though she might not have the tactfulness of her mother, who had been raised in New England. Beyond our student status, Cornelia and I shared our religious affiliation; she was a Catholic. Christianity in general was a great taboo at UC Berkeley, as my sense of prudence, well-trained in communist Poland, soon told me.

Cornelia soon fell prey to criticism by some of our graduate peers and she was referred to as "poor Cornelia and her religion," even though she never proselytized her religious convictions. The anti-Catholic bias that existed at UC Berkeley helped me understand the Catholicism of America. The Catholic university ministry, located in Newman Hall on College and Dwight, seemed to me at first guilt-driven, trying to repair the image that Catholicism imparted in this country for centuries. It required a great deal of adjustment to comprehend the motivation behind continuous challenges to the official Catholic teachings by the clergy seeking approval of a rather liberal congregation. Having grown up in an authoritarian culture, I learned as most people did, how to give to Caesar what was Caesar's, and lead my life in an accommodating mode. I never questioned the Church's teachings because I did not really know them in any depth. Like most people, I adopted my version of *sensus fidelium*, the sense of the faithful, that made my existence possible by adapting my faith to my life situation at the time of great social political upheaval in my native Poland.

Thus, I had remained a faithful churchgoer all my life, but more as an expression of my fidelity to the legacy of my parents and to my ethnic heritage rather than because of a genuine internal need for the divine. I did have a reverential sense of the sacred, but my spiritual life was numbed. My religious education did not animate my faith in the way that it would emanate with joy and praise. Rather, it was an external set of *ought not, ought to* that gave the direction to my life. My parents' fidelity to the Catholic Church had been essential for the crystallization of my attachment to the institution. An example was their anti-governmental stance present through their lives. My father prayed every evening for Poland's freedom from the Soviet occupation. My mother, as a school principal, had been asked to become a member of the ruling Communist Party to demonstrate her allegiance to the official ideology. She refused and was demoted to her previous status, which led to an early retirement, illness, and eventual death. Thus, I believe that my fidelity derives from my parents' sacrifice as a way of paying homage to them for who they had been.

My parents' commitment to the faith suddenly appeared debased by the form of Catholicism in America; a form that was alien to me. It took several years for me to understand the issues that were the focus of Catholicism at Newman Hall. During my first years, American Catholicism made little cultural sense to me. It sounded self-referential and imperialistic, ignoring anything that came before its way of living the faith, which made it very parochial after all. Just after confession, before Easter, when I received a white carnation as a symbol of the current state of my soul, from one of the parish stewards, I abandoned Newman Hall forever. The city of Berkeley parish, Saint Joseph the Worker, offered a Spanish mass where I found myself much more at home—until the awakening that came from my encounter with the Jesuits.

Berkeley culture often mocked Catholicism for all it represented; it saw in it a relic of the past that should have vanished from the surface of the earth a long time ago. That treatment of the Catholic Church was familiar. Paradoxically, I felt back in my element; I knew how to maneuver in ideologically murky waters thanks to my Polish upbringing. But Cornelia did suffer at Berkeley by being obliged to conceal her Catholic faith that constituted an important component of her identity in the multicultural landscape of the American campus. Moreover, she found little support from me, a fellow Catholic, who did not want to have anything to do with her parish, Newman Hall. What we both shared, however, was the understanding that we must remain closeted in the university environment that offered us a great educational opportunity. Our affinity lay in our shared God-given commitment to our beliefs; one that could not be easily eroded by peer pressure or the hostility of the dominating culture. Thus, if it was not a greatly enticing life of the local Church that caused the reversal of my academic fortune by diverting it from the road to the "pays de Cocagne," so, what was it then? I believe it was the Spirit of the Resurrected that showed me the road to Emmaus by progressively unveiling the directions through the voices of the masters. The Gospel of Luke (24:13-32) depicts the meeting of two disciples with the resurrected Jesus on on their way from Jerusalem to a village called Emmaus. Affected by Jesus's recent death, they cannot conceive of the fact that the traveler they just met might be Jesus. They invite him to join them for supper. During the meal Jesus reenacts the breaking of bread from their last supper together. Only then do they recognize the identity of the traveler who soon disappears. I see in this story a metaphor for my own journey, my own road to Emmaus which in my case was the road to Berkeley. On that road I met Christ who revealed himself through literature that taught me the value of making an unconditional commitment to the truth.

The beginning of my ascent toward academic laurels and subsequently to the turn of religious life was, nevertheless, filled with frustrations. To my surprise I found out that the program was very small; I was the only one admitted to it that year. Moreover, since the program was administered by the Spanish department, students who declared French as their first language were not very welcome in either department. The Spanish department favored those who would work closely with its own professors and teach language courses in Spanish. The French department, on the other hand, preferred graduate students in French and favored them for financial aid and employment as graduate student instructors. I discovered that I was, yet again, in a bureaucratic limbo reminiscent of my experiences in Polish and French universities. I had an advisor assigned ex officio who showed a great deal of cynicism by leaving me basically to my own resourcefulness. Thus, the first semester I had to survive on my own material means: no financial assistance, no faculty mentoring.

I had some meager savings, mainly from the sale of our house in Poland after my departure that my aunt sold on my behalf. Elżbieta Wewiórska had smuggled the money to France for me on one of her trips to Poland in the eighties, hiding it in intimate parts of her wardrobe, risking imprisonment if caught at the Polish-German border. The amount converted into dollars on the black market would allow me to buy a used car in good condition. This money proved to be extremely helpful at this moment of my American journey. I had been trying to not to use it unless absolutely necessary, as it represented the significant sacrifice made by my parents in a very difficult economic reality of communist Poland. Now, I felt this was the time to put it to good use, thereby honoring my parents by remembering the importance of education to them. Therefore, while still pondering if I should use the money now, the Gospel's parable of the talents (Matthew 25:14-30; Luke 19:11-27) popped into my mind. The parable stages a master going on a journey who, before taking off, entrusts to three slaves respectively five talents, three, and one according to their abilities. The first two invest and maximize the amount they have received, the third hides his one talent and, when the master returns, he gives back just what he has been given. Compensating the first two slaves who have put their talents to good use, the master becomes infuriated and throws the third "worthless slave into the outer darkness; in that place there will be weeping and gnashing of teeth."[4]

I recalled the convoluted semantics of the word when I studied the etymology of the word "talent" with Mademoiselle Hasselman in the course of French historical phonetics at the Sorbonne: "talent" literally referred to "currency" and has come to signify eventually "natural predispositions." The association of the Sorbonne and of UC Berkeley, as well as the fact that I was about to resume a study of Old French and historical grammar, led to the conviction that this was the moment to overcome the uneasiness about spending the money that I had not earned, but rather see in it a gift that ought to be invested in the fertile field of great promise that UC Berkeley represented for me. Under the influence of the Gospel parable, I invested the little I had in my education.

In my application essay I declared my interest in studying medieval literature given my positive experience at San Francisco State University and also that I was acquainted with Professor Howard Bloch's books and articles. I enrolled, therefore, in "Reading Old French" taught by Professor Bloch, and in "The Internal History of French" with Professor Susanne Fleishman, and in the second semester Latin course. The Latin requirement in the RLL program was demanding. I did not have sufficient knowledge of the language to take a translation exam and opted to fulfill the Latin requirement through coursework—one upper division course satisfied it, but I was not ready yet to take it. I also audited a Spanish undergraduate introduction to the history of Spanish literature.

"Reading Old French" was exciting, particularly because of the personality of Professor Bloch, who presented the subject in a very fresh manner. His interpretation of medieval literature challenged the traditional philological scholarship and applied to medieval studies the methodology inspired by poststructuralist criticism. One of his most controversial approaches was to establish fantasist etymologies à la Isidore of Seville, the seventh-century author of *Etymologiae*, a compendium of the learning of Antiquity for the use of Christianity.[5] Another trademark of Professor Bloch's scholarship was his predilection for shocking our modern sensitivity. *Fabliaux*, a medieval genre, characterized by the excess of sexual and scatological obscenity, anticlericalism, antifeminism, widely incorporated by Chaucer and Boccaccio in their work, was one of his favorite subjects. I still remember the exam for the course that consisted of a translation from Old French into English or modern French. On the test, rarely occurring words were given translation in English. One of these words was "manure." Not knowing either the Old French word or its English equivalent (I was translating into modern French), I guessed the meaning from the context that spoke a great deal about excrement and bad smells. My translation was ultimately accurate.

The seminar on historical grammar (or the internal history of French as the instructor labeled it) was very challenging, probably the most challenging of the courses I took in graduate school. Professor Fleishman had high expectations, and my background in historical grammar from the Sorbonne was of little help. In her approach, clarity of presentation was essential and knowing rules of phonetic change was of no value. It soon became obvious that in the course there was a group of students who knew what the professor liked and that she was more attentive to their class comments and opinions than to the others'. Fortunately, I had earned enough of respectability not to share the fate of some of my female classmates who often shed tears after receiving discouraging comments for their work. Despite not being at ease with the instructor, I appreciated the pressure to be as clear as my mental capacities would allow me: this was the main benefit I gained from taking her classes. A year later, I took another course with her as an option to satisfy the requirement of Romance philology for my qualifying exams. I understood it was safer to strive to please Professor Fleishman in class, even if unsuccessfully, than to face her at the qualifying exams. Only after some years did I realize how much she had given to us, her students, despite our occasional discomfort and resistance to her uncompromising way of standing by her very high scholarly standards. During my last year at UC Berkeley, Professor Fleishman succumbed to a terrifying illness, leukemia, that ultimately took her life at the pinnacle of her scholarly career.

In retrospect, that first semester represented a genuine period of trial of my resilience, tenacity, and capacity to sustain my focus on studies, all the while not knowing what my financial situation might be for the next semester. Great support came from Jana Svoboda, the librarian of the French Department. She and her husband had escaped Czechoslovakia in 1968, after the Warsaw Pact's forces brutally intervened to stop the Czech attempt to reject communist rule.[6] I did not need to explain to her what it meant to seek success in a new country, and in a new culture. Jana knew the departmental politics extremely well and became my actual advisor. We devised a strategy to obtain a teaching assistantship for me the following semester. Following Jana's strategic plan, I knocked on several office doors explaining that if I did not have a teaching position, I'd not be able to continue with my graduate work. I never knew how, or who, helped to disentangle my precarious situation but knocking on the doors helped: I had my first teaching assignment for the next term, French I. I surmise that I received the assistantship thanks to

Richard Kern, who just started as the director of the lower division French program, and to the administrative assistant, who had a great deal of influence in deciding who would be employed.

To be approved to teach, I had to observe a pilot class for two semesters. The instructor of that class was Danièle Boucher, a lecturer from France with very Parisian manners. Danièle had a comical side to her: always running, or taking time finding the graded copies of students' homework in her bag (that contained half of her personal dossiers). In the classroom she had a cheerful sense of humor, which she expressed while personalizing her presentations by relating the current material to her students' context. Although sitting in Danièle's classes for two semesters was superfluous, the experience was useful for a neophyte teacher because it had some practical implications that helped me make ends meet. Danièle was delegated to observe my class a year later; she was pleased with my teaching and offered me a position to work with her in the summer intensive French language workshop. I accepted and participated for several consecutive summers. It was an extraordinary opportunity to boost my modest income, and even afford to travel to Europe.

Earning my living as well as providing for my studies through teaching French became the norm. Even though I came to America with an idea of shedding my early adulthood in Paris, it seems that circumstances caused me to remain *with* French and *in* French, therefore this time was marked by challenges, frustrations, and doubt, I wanted to renew myself without French. But as I had discovered, my fate had been sealed, and in my social and professional circles I remained associated with France. Moreover, I surprised myself by gravitating more and more toward Paris as my cultural and social reference. The more I enjoyed Berkeley the more I desired to share that joy with my former social circles in Paris. My American friends drifted away, following their business demands, and gradually our contacts became more and more sporadic.

The renewed closeness to French did not prevent me from flirting with Spanish which led me to the class with Professor Charles Faulhaber, "Medieval Love Literature of Spain." It represented another connection to the great scholarship in Romance Languages. Professor Faulhaber's class was extremely demanding with regard to the volume of required readings, but he infused students with energy and enthusiasm that made us maintain the tempo and expectations of his syllabus. The course explored the motif of love in a wide range of literary production of the Middle Ages. The most memorable discovery were *kharjas*, short lyrical stanzas written in Arabic or in the emerging Romance dialect of the Iberian Peninsula, also known as Mozarabic. *Kharjas* are believed to be the oldest recorded instances of lyric poetry in any Romance language dating back to the eleventh century. Studying these poems were reminiscent of my travels to Spain while still living in Paris. Scenes from Valencia, Toledo, Seville, Cadiz, and Granada returned to me vividly—with their past as a part of Al-Andalus, the Moorish state on the Iberian Peninsula from roughly the eighth century up to the fall of the Kingdom of Granada to the Catholic Kings, Isabel and Ferdinand's rule in 1492. The poets' longing voice in *kharjas* revived my own experience of longing for "more," that was inspired by the estranging beauty of the Spanish landscape, that was exhausted by the drought of torrid summers, expressing thirst for the elusive *something* that a life, out of my reach, stimulated desire and generated illusions while seeking to compensate for the absence of fulfillment.

Toward the end of the term, I was ready to make the final jump from French to Spanish. I spoke to Professor Faulhaber about it, but he explained that there were fewer RLL students majoring in French as their first field than in Spanish, therefore it was better for the program if students were more evenly distributed among the languages.

This advice indeed sealed my covenant with French. I was disappointed, but then reflected and realized that French had been part of my consciousness for twenty years, since that first "Bonjour" in high school. The fact that English, with its imperialistically pragmatic claims on everything that does not surrender to its linguistic and cultural paradigm, did not expunge French from my nearly daily usage, was telling me that I needed to accept this situation and stop fleeing that which had become an integral part of who I was. I thought of the female protagonist of the Polish novel by Maria Dąbrowska, *Noce i dnie* [*Nights and Days*], who often contemplates the possibility of walking out of her marriage to the man she thinks she does not love. It is only at the time of his terminal illness that she realizes that all these movements of the heart—rejection, repulsion, attempts to flee, subsequent returns because there is no better alternative—constitute the essence on which she has built her existence. At her husband's deathbed she finally understands the value of remaining in her marriage. Only then does she accept her marriage as a real thing, giving up fantasies about a romantic relationship that actually never materialized.[7]

In the process of that reconciliation with my personal *francophonie*, I signed up for the seminar on Old Provençal poetry with Professor Joseph Duggan. The subject complemented my medieval interests and related to French culture was not French *sensu stricto*. Professor Duggan, a very popular teacher, is an internationally recognized scholar for his edition of *The Song of Roland*,[8] as well as his study of the Spanish medieval epic *El Cid*.[9] In the classroom, he had the gift for creating a congenial atmosphere, often telling anecdotes from his rich academic career. The positive classroom atmosphere only facilitated an otherwise extensive amount of hard work required to meet high demands of the course. We had to study the grammar and lexicon of this new difficult language whose verbal forms were not regularized and could vary slightly from poet to poet. We were also expected to translate the poems, preferably into English, as some students in the course, who specialized in comparative literature, had not mastered modern French well enough. And, I was learning both English and the twelfth-century Provençal.

The most surprising element of the course was Professor Duggan's intellectual challenge to the concept of "distant love," personified by Jaufré Rudel.[10] Professor Duggan demonstrated, very convincingly with many examples, that this promoter of "love from afar" was an exception, rather than a representative of the whole of the Troubadours' poetry. The myth of courtly love, or, the worship of a distant, inaccessible woman, was elaborated on later. The first Troubadour William IX of Poitiers [Guillen de Peiteus] represented the perfect counter example to Jaufré Rudel's stance. Professor Duggan provided us with a convincing selection of poetized examples of his sexual prowess. One of these is about the Ladies with a cat [Farai un vers, po mi somelh] that contains amusing sexual innuendoes recounting the poet's adventure with the wives of two noblemen. The suggestive presence of a read-haired cat in the midst of the fornicators gives the poem a comical frame,

> Per la coa de mantenen
> Tira-l gat et el escoissen:
> Plajas mi feron mais de cen
> Aquella ves
> Mas eu no-m mogra ges enguers
> Qui m'ausizes.[11]

> ["And all at once, they yanked his tail
> To make him dig in, tooth and nail;
> I got a hundred scars, wholesale,
> Right then and there.
> They could have flayed me, though, before
> I'd budge one hair"][12]

With this example and a few others, the myth of an idealized love, that found its most sublimated form in the fourteenth century in Petrarch's sonnets to Laura,[13] was convincingly dismissed. That annoyed me because in those years my sentimental pendulum had clearly swung over to the Jaufré Rudel-Petrarch philosophy of "distant love." I wished the opinion of distant love had been confirmed, so I could agree with Petrarch's "Letter to Posterity" in which he writes, "I struggled in my younger days with a keen but constant and pure attachment, and would have struggled with it longer had not the sinking flame been extinguished by death—premature and bitter, but salutary. I should be glad to be able to say that I had always been entirely free from irregular desires, but I should lie if I did so."[14] In my case it was a metaphorical death—the death caused by the choice of the values conditioned by the culture of the place, America. American culture invites humanity to pursue happiness through personal development and often requires severing human burdensome ties. Yet, I do relate to Petrarch's self-imposed solitude and appreciation of lonesomeness that offers the luxury of personal growth that a shared life would not have. By the time I studied the Troubadours, I had been used to this mode of solitary self-seeking that I could hardly exchange for any other situation. Notwithstanding, that "blow" to my comfort zone of lonesomeness from Professor Duggan's perspective, I enjoyed his course very much.

Freed from bonds of close friendships, reconciled with my *francophone* self, and now better adapted to the university's expectations, I was in full speed ahead for the *pays de Cocagne*.

Chapter Eight

From Illusion to the Truth

Three years of coursework passed by rapidly, and the time came for politically strategizing for the qualifying PhD exams and choosing a dissertation director. Following advice from my peers, I enrolled in an undergraduate course on Renaissance literature with Professor Timothy Hampton. I was told he was an engaging teacher and bright scholar. It was true. I audited the class for a few meetings and was particularly taken by the fact that he was able to extract from texts elements that were engaging to the modern-day reader. The approach contrasted greatly with non-hermeneutic, merely plain historical approaches, similar to those I had encountered in Poland and France, making the historically remote period hardly accessible and, above all, extremely dull. The best example of that contrast was the sixteenth-century poet Clément Marot whose poetry I had read in the past, and had the effect of a sleeping pill. Professor Hampton had a gift for highlighting the aspects of Marot's poetry that made it actually engaging, mainly because the background of the turbulent social and political landscape led to the rise of the Protestant Reformation.

But it was the study of François Rabelais's *Pantagruel* that caused my admiration for the professor, and my interest in the course. Although I had read *Gargantua* and *Pantagruel* at San Francisco State, with some interest, it was now that I was actually exposed to the richness and complexity of the work.[1] After reading Edwin Duval's study, *The Design of Rabelais's Pantagruel*, I chose to write a paper on *Pantagruel*'s underlying messianic design.[2] I was delighted that the book had a Christian-friendly interpretation as opposed to those readings that interpreted Rabelais as a militant atheist or a revolutionary anti-clerical herald who trampled all tradition. Whereas Rabelais certainly mocks the excesses of his time, he never undermines the foundations of the Western Christian heritage. Reading other interpretations of

Rabelais's texts, such as Terence Cave's *The Cornucopian Text* or Mikhail Bakhtin's *Rabelais and His World*, only made Duval's argument more persuasive.[3] Cave's conclusions certainly helps elucidate the process of writing and the intentions behind Rabelais's prolific prose. As for Bakhtin's notorious interpretation of Rabelais that sees his writing as essentially indebted to folk culture in its carnival esthetics, I found it unconvincing, and after reading Duval, I agreed that there was too much humanist erudition in *Pantagruel* to credit it with so much folk influence and dismissed that interpretation altogether. When I teach *Pantagruel* to undergraduate students now, I start by referencing Sacha Baron Cohen's film *Borat*.[4] Students immediately detect the satirical intentions of the author.

Pantagruel further stimulated my reconciliation with French literary heritage. Through its satire of institutions such as the Sorbonne, the judicial system, the medical profession, and the linguistic snobbism of the Parisians, *Pantagruel* helped me build a critical distance toward the French and France. I was certainly receptive to its benign outlook on human failure in an attempt to reach the ideals fabricated by political and social institutions which have unrealistic expectations for fulfillment. Rabelais had the sense of irony of a great humanist who foresaw unavoidable failures in the pursuit of ideals. This is probably what Bakhtin sensed when, confronted with ideological chimeras of the Soviet social realism, he read Rabelais. The author of *Pantagruel* offers us a lesson in humility and invites those who tend to frown on human weakness to accept the limitations of human potential and opt for laugher rather than resentment.

The course eased whatever remained of my misgivings to keep French as my first field and solidified the foundation for further studies with Professor Hampton. I abandoned my intention to specialize in the medieval period because the prospect of finding an academic position as a medievalist was scant and elected the early modern. The encounter with Professor Hampton was determining, and, therefore, I opted for the field that would allow me to have him as my dissertation director. Moreover, I discovered that he was also a faculty member in the Department of Italian Studies and had written studies on Torquato Tasso, the author of a celebrated poem in his time, *Gerusalemme liberata* [*Jerusalem Delivered*].[5]

In the period preceding the required oral doctoral examination, I enrolled in a course with Professor Jacqueline Lichtenstein on Pierre Corneille and Aristotle's *Poetics*.[6] I was reluctant to take it given my past experience with teachers trained in France but I decided to give it a try; it turned out to be one of the most influential academic encounters. Professor Lichtenstein was a professor of philosophy, teaching one semester a year at the University of Paris X-Nanterre, and one semester a year at UC Berkeley. Above all, she was a free spirit. The course started by the announcement, "You know the topic, I don't have a syllabus, but even if I had one, I would not follow it."

We soon understood what that meant when she started lecturing. It was a performance in itself. From one concept she was able to elaborate a clear presentation that was logical and associative. In this way she was able to construct her lecture in front of us, the audience, thanks to a particular training she must have received, mixed with a personal talent. One of her favorite phrases was "maintenant j'ouvre une parenthèse" [now I am opening a parenthesis], and she could go off topic to a related topic, broadening our perspective on the intellectual history of Europe. It was absolutely fascinating to pursue that flow of thought that never lost its initial premise, even though it might have wandered off at some point during the mental process. Her knowledge of art history and aesthetics that shaped modes of representation were astonishingly broad. Most importantly for me, she placed the work of Corneille in the realm of early modern philosophical debates on art and literature. It was a far-reaching perspective, going back to the Renaissance debates surrounding the *Poetics* of Aristotle, when the humanists of the period rediscovered and avidly discussed it. With astonishment, I discovered that the French Academy was actually an offspring of Italian practices; each major city in Italy had an *academia* to pronounce judgments on cultural trends and changes. Now, if we blame the French Academy for its rigidity regarding the rules for French language usage, and for being the main denunciator of Corneille's seventeenth-century aesthetic liberties in his most popular play *Le Cid*, the blame ought to go to the Italians as well, a fact that is often ignored.[7] While fascinated by the culture of Hollywood, Professor Lichtenstein was able to make a case, with examples of the early modern intellectual debates, that the art, grounded in philosophical principles was superior to the art that merely aimed to entertain rather than seek the truth in representation. Each lecture would have a "pause-cigarette" on a balcony of the building where the class met. When we saw Professor Lichtenstein pulling the packet of cigarettes from her bag, we were concerned that she might either activate the fire alarm or incur a fine for ignoring the fresh anti-tobacco laws enacted at the heyday of the anti-tobacco campaign on campus.

The encounter with Professor Lichtenstein determined the choice of my dissertation topic. Until hearing her introduction to Corneille's work, reading a Corneille play would compare to watching paint dry, after learning about the background of the early modern philosophical disputes, Corneille's theater turned out to be very exciting. Additionally, knowing that Professor Hampton had a chapter on Corneille in one of his books, I was more and more inclined to make Corneille a central figure of my dissertation.

Most influential for me was that Professor Lichtenstein opened the door to not only the intellectual but also the spiritual reality that stirred my excitement. In speaking about Corneille's introduction to theater, she mentioned the impact of Jesuit education in his early formation. The Jesuit pedagogical approach to the instruction of philosophy and morals, widely used theater as its messenger.

Jesuits often wrote plays themselves for their pupils to perform. In the course, I also learned about the scholarship of Marc Fumaroli who explores Jesuit heritage in Western culture.[8] The mention of the Jesuits brought back memories from the Petit Collège of the Saint-Louis de Gonzague School in Paris, where before Christmas and Easter, *le père Desbains* directed students in the *Mysteries of Christ's Life*, or other plays with pedagogical purposes. The conflation of that period of my life with this new development infused me with renewed energy necessary to face the dissertation stage.

Given the connection between Italy and France, which Professor Lichtenstein made so clear, little by little the idea of a comparative dissertation topic emerged. Moreover, Professor Hampton's scholarly interest also lay in the Franco-Italian connection. The following semester he offered a comparative literature seminar on poetic epics, in which I discovered Torquato Tasso's *Gerusalemme liberata* and Ludovico Ariosto's *Orlando furioso*.[9] These two Renaissance epic poems epitomize the debate about good and bad art. In his appropriation of Aristotle's *Poetics*, Tasso sets the foundation for the neoclassical doctrine,[10] whereas Ariosto consciously subverts the rules of verisimilitude by giving free rein to his imagination. *Orlando furioso* chants the fictitious deeds of Charlemagne's knights and most prominently of his knight Orlando (the Roland of the famous French medieval epic). While indeed very imaginative and witty, with the purpose to challenge the rising proponents of neoclassical ideal in esthetics, the poem seemed to me as *over-the-top* in its constant change of the setting, making it difficult to understand who is who in the plot, let alone the flying horses and a trip to the moon. I did not have difficulty aligning with a side in the debate. An additional reason for my rejection of Ariosto's esthetics might have been its shoddy appeal to the audience's demand for entertainment, strangely reminiscent of modern-day television's strategy that, in the opinion of many, aims to exploit the masses' appetite for diversion and distraction. While reading *Orlando*, I could not help thinking about the television series *Xena: Warrior Princess*.[11] Formative lessons from my friendship with Jane Dickenson, in discarding the distracting impact of television entertainment, must have come into play when I was to define my dissertation topic. Among the *isms* in vogue at that time, New Historicism appealed to me as the least dogmatic as well as the least jargon-loaded. I particularly appreciated the freedom that came from the assumption that all we can do about historical facts is to interpret them through the lenses of who we have become under the pressures of the historical contingencies of our own times.[12] I soon learned that my dissertation committee would not have any major problems with this approach. So, I undertook what was to become a rather long interaction with three early modern authors whose work I intended to compare. I proposed to study their efforts to comply with esthetic and moral ideals of their time and expose their ineluctable failure to meet the standards. The title of my project was "A

Historicization of an Ideal: Poetic Practice in the Work of Three Counter Reformation Writers, Torquato Tasso, Pierre Corneille, and Lope de Vega."

Tasso's scorn for art as sheer entertainment of the masses corresponded to my own attitude of disdain for popular culture (even though we both failed to resist its appeal at all times. I have a weak spot for Elvis and Adele in my heart). On the basis of Aristotle's *Poetics*, Tasso elaborated high standards of art grounded in rational principles, yet his hypersensitivity and erotic inclinations are never absent from his poetic work. For modern readers, accustomed to mass entertainment sold by television culture, Tasso's scrupulosity in seeking art that would render the orderliness of the world in its didactic principles seems cumbersome and drab. Nevertheless, he epitomizes the courage to contest fashionable trends through a staunch commitment to intellectual quality, at the expense of popularity. Despite his scorn of entertainment, paradoxically, Tasso eventually gained great popularity, and not because of his defense of high art, but because of the numerous adaptations of romantic motifs in his poems that, in fact,he considered inferior features. Reading his works, be it the *Discorsi dell'arte poetica*, the play *Aminta* or *Gerusalemme liberata*, I found in Tasso a soul mate.[13] He was as conflicted as I was in my inclination to indulge in the bountiful hedonistic pleasures in Berkeley that filled the shelves of its health conscious facilities and markets. On the other hand, I never forgot from where I came and that there was another world still striving to rebuild from the abuses of the subjugation to an ideology that turned out to be extremely harmful. If this world was created by a just God, I thought, it was not right to give in to good fortune and take advantage of the moment. Berkeley was for me the happy turn of the Wheel of Fortune, but I was too conscious of the impossibility of that state to last. Tasso appealed to that awareness of the fragile equilibrium set by human strife. He stimulated in me the need to transcend the happiness of the moment, perhaps because of a catastrophism drunk with my mother's milk in the gloom of the communist reality. The "pays de Cocagne" was not to be my destination, I realized in the solitude of my studies while attempting to draft a coherent proposal in view of positive appraisal by my dissertation readers. Tasso's notion of *altri diletti* [other pleasures] at the outset of his great poem, *Gerusalemme liberata* coincided with my bent to self-indulgence in the bountiful Berkeley.[14]

As I was trying to contain my penchant for *altri diletti* and discipline myself in order to make progress on my dissertation work, "The Allegory of the Poem" that Tasso included at the conclusion of his poem spoke to me like a spiritual master trying to help a disciple overcome inner confusion by conquering attachments to worldly things that have no real value. The author clarifies the purpose of his work as a metaphorical illustration of human strife toward "felicity," epitomized by the city of Jerusalem to be conquered by the domination of irascible forces. "This felicity is a good very difficult to pursue, being placed atop the steep and wearying hill of Virtue, and toward it are directed, as toward an ultimate goal, all the actions of political man."[15] The idea of self-conquest while living in Berkeley seemed, at first, as difficult as the conquest of Jerusalem in the eleventh century. The culture of the city, inspired by New Age trends and philosophies, identified any attempts to master one's effort to restrict hedonistic impulses as repression. Predominantly materialistic literary criticism of Tasso's work pointed out his social inadaptability at a time of diverse conflicts in sixteenth-century Italy. Psychoanalytical readings suggested paranoia induced by the split with the Christendom that Tasso feared, particularly in face of the territorial gains of the Ottoman Empire.

For me, a Catholic survivor, who has never lost the notion of sin, of my own inadequacy, and of a providential presence of a force that brought me to that point of life—I saw in Tasso a companion who understood my misgivings about the pursuit of fulfillment within the criteria dictated by the academic ethos. I was not interested in Tasso's neurosis caused by religious conflict, nor did I smile indulgently as did atheist critics at his failings in purging his poem of overtly sensuous motifs. Tasso explains further in "The Allegory," "Because of the imperfections of the human nature and the deceits of its antagonist, man does not arrive at this felicity without many inward difficulties or without finding along the way many external impediments—all which are portrayed for us by the figure of the poem."[16] It was the insight about interiority, about the soul that I found most valuable in Tasso.

The metaphor was helpful at this stage of my life when in doubt about the value of undertaking the lengthy path toward the completion of my PhD, I became convinced that, although trends in literary criticism were useful tools for analyzing and understanding literature, they, in fact, represented half-truths, not to say deception, about the value of genuine literary work. Tasso's thoughts convinced me that he was intellectually seeking something that could not be easily contained within a paradigm of an ideological literary criticism that tried to encapsulate, in limited thought, the expanse of his message about human nature.

At the time I read Tasso for my dissertation, I was not familiar with Jesuit spirituality. Nevertheless, Tasso's visualization of the human person had a methodic appeal that showed signs of a well-integrated philosophical and spiritual paradigm. I read in his biography that he studied under the Jesuits who had recently opened their college in Naples. Then, not being familiar with Jesuit spirituality, I did not make a connection between this influence and Tasso's visualized representation of the mature man, which I could only appreciate years later as a practitioner of the Jesuit spiritual method.

Yet, even without an explicit familiarity with Jesuit spiritual imagination, Tasso's poem, accompanied with its allegory, had an impact on me. At the time of existential questioning, it invited me to look at my own life with all its contradictions: a life in prey of entangled desires, and of high aspirations for excellence, sometimes extinguished by my lack of perseverance. Where was my Jerusalem to be conquered? Who were the real enemies that I encountered on my way to civic felicity, the place in the world I would find peace? With Tasso's help I realized that most of these enemies resided in me, in my own *ozio* [idleness] as Tasso would have it.[17] This visualization of my own humanity, following Tasso's allegory, with my circular errance, my angers, my flights, and my dwelling in the places that fed my selfishness, helped me to reconsider the value of the whole academic enterprise. I needed to find deviation from the current predicament which mainstream academic culture encouraged me to embrace. But, I did not know yet, how, and where.

As a survival strategy, I adopted the attitude of fording the stream rather than swimming in full immersion, a practice I learned in communist Poland, hoping that I might eventually reach the shore of a land of plenty beyond the confines of the artifice of academia. I read most of the recommended nihilistic critiques that interpreted Tasso's work as the fruit of a profound emotional unbalance due to a split between his uncritical allegiance to the Counter-Reformation Church and the rise of Protestant modernity, that was to sweep the entire world in its claim to the manifest destiny of conquest and empire. But I intended to preserve what I sensed, intuitively in the bottom of my heart, to be the irreducible truth contained in his depiction of the human person. Human nature, as he sees it, is a dynamic entity, incomplete without God's grace, often falling prey to inner weaknesses, aggravated by external unfavorable circumstances. I immediately felt this truth reflected in my life. The authoritative, persuasive clarity with which Tasso wrote, armed me "spiritually" for the remaining time of solitary struggles with the topic of my dissertation, and above all, with myself during this journey through an uncharted territory. The connection between Jesuit spirituality and Tasso's work did not come to the surface at this time; I was exposed to it much later. Only while reflecting on that period from an interiorized Jesuit perspective, could I say that the text worked through me, and then led me into the direction of the metaphorical Jerusalem, a civic felicity I desired to conquer by finding a place in society that would appease my longing for more than the conventional felicity of bourgeois society—either in its French version of *petit peu*, or a Californian call for more. Tasso's writings worked on me like white magic pointing me toward the realm that lay above the political realm of academic debates: a realm of the truth about human nature and its purpose in this world. The text worked like salutary medicine making me see my own idleness, becoming an easy target for a world that has lost the sense of commitment to the truth, replacing it with the political compromise of the bourgeois capitalist mentality in power—more euphemistically called the middle class with its paradisiac ideal of the "pays de Cocagne."

Of course, studying these questions on the UC Berkeley campus, with its tradition of fighting for individual freedom against bourgeois culture and the state's aspirations to control the student body, was both exciting and inciting.

But the struggle for very meaningful causes, such as the right to free speech, belonged to the past. It appeared to me that the issues fought for by the campus activists were relatively jejune when compared with the problems of the rest of the world in the 1990s. One of the heated topics of the day was the fight by a student for the right to attend class in the nude. He was cheered and supported by a group of Berkeley residents called the "Explicit Players." Elsewhere in the world there were many instances of war, a civil war in Rwanda, various terrorist attacks on western interests, including domestic terrorism in Oklahoma, and a major earthquake in Los Angeles. The university life remained unaffected by the horrors of the day continued its life infatuated with its own myth of the champion of progress on the planet. Literary criticism continued its pseudo-involvement in the life of the polity, creating its own discursive screen which it claimed to be the only real thing that mattered, just as if Disney World created a reality purged of the truth. Individualism and cliquishness voiced their claims to their own particular truths with an outcome of breeching the social fabric of the community. Passions, with desires for individual happiness, unleashed their demands, overshadowing the world of abject suffering that was inflicted by hate or incomprehensible fate. How many people in the world pray for their *petit peu* of subsistence and cannot obtain it, all the while campus activists and intellectuals multiply dreams and claims, demanding their superfluous, unrestrained *more*?

Tasso became my closest companion in this period of doubts and discouragement. His ideas have worked as that bitter medicine he speaks of at the inception of his poem. I swallowed it, coated with the lure of an eventual prestigious academic career. Yet, it permeated my soul and produced disdain for all these worldly values of academic success by unveiling their emptiness. Tasso renders, metaphorically, the way that temptation enters the human psyche and subsequently overpowers the person by contaminating the rational faculties of the soul. The main symbolic agent of seduction in *Gerusalemme liberata* is Armida, a Sarasin princess whose beauty is used by the satanic forces to awaken desire in the Christian knights as she manages to penetrate their camp and walks through it to meet the commander Godfrey.

> Mostra il bel petto le sue nevi ignude,
> onde il foco d'Amor si nutre e desta.
> Parte appar de le mamme acerbe e crude,
> parte altrui ne ricopre invida vesta:
> invida, ma s'a gli occhi il varco chiude,
> l'amoroso pensier già non arresta,
> ché non ben pago di bellezza esterna
> ne gli occulti secreti anco s'interna.[18]

> [Her lovely bosom displays its naked snows by which the flame of Love is awakened and fed; a portion appears of her breasts unripe and unready, a portion the envious vesture hides from others: envious but if to the eyes it

closes the path, it does not wholly check the amorous mind, which—being not well content with outward beauty—works itself still within to the hidden secrets.][19]

Armida's strategy is effective as she eventually manages to seduce the worthiest knight of the Christian army, the right hand of Godfrey, Rinaldo whom she transports to an enchanted island where he looses his manly valor as he indulges in all of the pleasures that the lovely maid is skilled to provide. In the entire allegorical scheme of the poem, Rinaldo is meant to represent the irascible faculty of the soul, Plato's category from *Republic*, whose role is to work in the service of reason by defending it against the concupiscent faculties of the soul.[20] When the irascible faculty disobeys reason, it works on behalf of concupiscence and causes damage to the interests of the soul by dulling its defenses. In the poem, Armida succeeds temporarily in numbing the alertness of Rinaldo until his companions manage to penetrate the island and, unnoticed by the sleeping Armida, show him his unmanly reflection on his shield. Ashamed, he recovers his countenance and flees Armida, who, in the meantime has fallen victim to her own snare: she has fallen in love with Rinaldo to the extent that, discovering his disappearance, she is heartbroken and attempts suicide.

While figuring out the meaning of the Armida episode in order to include it in my dissertation, I could not help thinking of my own life in Berkeley as a life on an enchanted island. The beauty of the landscape, the mildness of the climate, the good food available in health-conscious stores, and finally, the prestige of the university of which I was part, all led to a happy alienation whose wellbeing I could not bear anymore. My Polish irascible faculty of the soul had betrayed me. I needed a Rinaldo-type of epiphany. Given my cultural background, I felt I had no right to the comfort I had been enjoying. I needed to reach out to the world that did not have the privilege of being sheltered from the truth. And, that truth was the *truth of the cross*.

The period spent writing the chapter on Tasso instilled guilt in me for what I perceived as the undeserved wellbeing I was enjoying. I realized that my life in Berkeley represented more than the *petit peu* about which I had fantasized during my meager Parisian years. The Spirit of fame painted phantasms of an academic career. It whispered to me, encouraging the temptation to adorn my discourse with more fashionable references, ones that would open the doors to the salons susceptible to include me in their network. I did some of it to assure my graduation, but I resisted surrendering to academic pressure groups. Tasso brought back the critical stance toward culture that Simone Weil's *La Pesanteur et la grâce* had infused in me at a very formative moment.[21]

Once I drafted the Tasso chapter, I began my chapter on Corneille. The communion with Corneille appealed to my sense of duty that I believe was transmitted to me by my father's genes and which I recognize little by little as I age. The textbook interpretation of Cornelian heroism set an exemplarity of virtue that I found appealing. The heroes and heroines of Corneille's plays never succumb to the weaknesses induced by passion. They always find *superhuman* inner strength to master their inclinations that, if unharnessed, would lead them astray from their commitment to the common good. The play *Horace* elevates the heroic ethos to the heights of ideological purism. The title character sacrifices everything for the emerging Roman state: he kills best friend, a native of the rival city of Alba, and his own sister, who chooses her personal happiness rather than surrendering to the ever-growing demands of the state. In a soliloquy the protagonist Horace expresses his zealous commitment to the service of the state,

> Contre qui que ce soit que mon pays m'emploie,
> J'accepte aveuglement cette gloire avec joie;
> Celle de recevoir de tells commandements
> Doit étouffer en nous tous autres sentiments. [22]

> [No matter against whom my country picks me
> I blindly greet this glory with acclaim;
> The fame of having won this rare command
> Should stifle every feeling in us.] [23]

Commentators, like Simone Weil, have criticized Corneille for the inhumanity, if not monstrosity, of the heroic ideal that *Horace* represents. In *The Need for Roots*, Weil expresses harsh judgment with respect to Corneille's forceful advocacy of heroism, "Corneille himself is an excellent example of the sort of asphyxia which seizes Christian morality when it comes in contact with the Roman Spirit."[24]

Had not I been writing my chapter in America, I would have likely embraced Weil's criticism. However, I was writing it on the enchanted island of Berkeley. The island had given me the illusion of freedom that was becoming unbearable. Beyond the horizon of the island lay Oakland and Richmond, California, two cities with a vivid memory of the past, on which the freedom to do what one pleases was born. Oakland and Richmond have a predominantly African American population, a reminder of the not so free displacement of people of color. We face here an unsurpassable paradox: Berkeley, with its cult of everything free, is an economic offspring of the sweat of the laborers of the past that contributed to the capital of this island. And now the island pretends to live a perennial guilt-free paradise. In the dénouement of *Horace*, the king expresses the truth about the construction of political reality. A polity feeds on ideological dissimulation. It must dissimulate the foundational violence in order to bring up the semblance of original innocence. Therefore, the *enchanted island* of Berkeley denies any association with broader America, and yet, very much like Disney World's hyperreality, it camouflages its links to the universal horror by denouncing it elsewhere, except, of course, in its own neck of the woods. As Corneille's king lucidly states, defending Horace's fratricidal crimes,

> De pareils serviteurs sont les forces des rois,
> Et de pareils aussi sont au-dessus des lois,
> Qu'elles se taisent donc, que Rome dissimule
> Ce que dès sa naissance elle vit en Romule:
> Elle peut bien souffrir en son libérateur
> Ce qu'elle a bien souffert en son premier auteur.[25]

> [Such servants are very sap of kings,
> And therefore such are held above the law.
> Let law be silent then, and Rome be blind
> To what she saw in Romulus at her birth:
> She may well suffer in her liberator
> What she bore meekly in her founding father.][26]

The king invites those who point the finger at Horace's killings to remember that the fratricidal murder of Romulus perpetrated on his brother Remus constitutes the foundation of Rome. Thus the present wellbeing of Rome is founded on past horrors. By the same token, Berkeley's earthly felicity cannot be dissociated from the history of the entire nation; it is convenient but hypocritical to condemn capitalism and imperialism while taking full advantage of its legacy. While criticizing Berkeley, I also realized my own sinking—into the seductive charm of the oblivion induced by the beauty of the natural setting, delicious food, and cultural offerings.

I needed a wakeup call, a mirror, like Rinaldo's shield, to bring me back from my narcissistic existence that allowed me to roll in idleness. I had no right to live on the enchanted island where Fortune placed me. Thinking how to resist the charm and how to escape from the spell of easy living in Berkeley, it occurred to me that Tasso and Corneille were both pupils of the Jesuits. How would this upbringing forge their worldview that advocated the rejection of the transient values in search for an otherworldly ideal that politics tended to mask? My own past affiliation with the Jesuits in Paris became more present. While working on the Corneille chapter, I also audited a course on Descartes with a professor from New York University, Timothy Reiss, and here again the Jesuit influence of La Flèche surfaced. Marc Fumaroli's scholarship indicates that the Jesuits influenced education in early Europe. These confluences of the Jesuit motif in my existence at that time were revelatory and pulled me in a new direction.

Nevertheless, I was resisting the impulse to explore that reality since in secularized and anticlerical society the word "Jesuit" has been, at best, an ambiguous term. Suppressions and revolutions resulted in confiscations of the institutions, replacing the label "Jesuit" with secular equivalents, while adopting the methods without acknowledging any debts to the tradition. "Jesuit" became associated with "Jesuitical," with a quite negative connotation of cunning, plotting, and secrecy. Little by little, I acquiesced to my rising curiosity about the Jesuit tradition, discovering that major writers and intellectuals, such Molière and Voltaire, benefited greatly from their Jesuit education. As I reflected on Corneille's conversion to "good" art, the Jesuit influence transpired more and more. Tasso, Corneille, and my third author, Félix Lope de Vega, were all educated by Jesuit institutions. There was a common denominator in them: a quest for helping humanity to live in harmony in community, by understanding and accepting the necessary constraints that the common good demands of all who choose a communal path of living. The common good requires the learned and habituated ability to control the appetites and passions that, if allowed to run freely, may end up being destructive for not only the subject, but also for community. This is the main lesson from Tasso's ideas and their elaborate and gallicized version of Corneille. Of course, these ideas are not brand-new. They derive from ancient philosophy, transmitted through the humanist corpus of the Jesuit schools' curricula. Tasso's ideal of civic felicity was metaphorically represented as the city of Jerusalem, and the ideal could be achieved through self-conquest in view of a harmonious coexistence of diverse human temperaments that all restrain their personal desires to serve the common good. With these thinkers, we are far from the libertarian right to individuality with little collective accountability to the common good. Contrary to the modern idea of the antagonistic relationship between the political power and the individual, these early modern thinkers, mistrustful of human nature, saw in the political power an ally to civic felicity. In his play *Le Cid*, Corneille expresses the role of the absolutist government in the king's words,

> Un roi dont la prudence a de meilleurs objets
> Est meilleur ménager du sang de ses sujets:
> Je veille pour les miens, mes soucis les conservent,
> comme le chef a soin des membres qui le servent.[27]

> [A king whose wisdom harbors better aims
> Can husband better his subjects' blood:
> I cherish mine, I take care to preserve it,
> Just as the head cares for the limbs that serve it.][28]

As in *Gerusalemme liberata* here again we notice the organic metaphor of the body politic. While Tasso focuses on individual self-conquest, Corneille is interested in the political extension of the idea of the mastery of individualistic tendencies to the service of the body politic. The political power is represented as an exemplary case of such mastery to be trusted by the subject.

From this perspective, a glance at American society, with its claims not to civic felicity but to flourishing individualism, appeared to me in a very particular light. In fact, thanks to this ideal guaranteed by the political system, I felt unbearably fulfilled and happy in my status as a graduate student on a major American campus facing the prospect of influencing, after graduation, the intellectual life, not only of this country but ultimately of the world. Yet, was this true happiness? My regular summer trips to France, made possible by my modest graduate student instructor's wages, kept my connection with France and French alive. Overseas, my friends remained faithful to me; sometimes I did not share with some of them the news of my visit, for fear of hurting their feelings because I was not physically able to see all of them within the time limits of my stay. I appreciated the slower mobility of French society, and Paris looked nearly the same with only a few new additions.

During one of these visits, I lost a filling and needed to see a dentist. I called Dr. Fredj, my Parisian dentist, who I had not seen for more than ten years, and who had rescued my teeth from the impact of Polish socialized medicine after our Jewish dentist moved to Israel. Dr. Fredj got to know me well, given the neglect of my dental care. He was a *pied noir* with a wonderful sense of humor and loved to make me laugh while I was supposed to keep my mouth wide-open. He would call me jokingly and affectionately "Monsieur Mokati." On that visit, after years of not seeing me, he said something of the sort, "Monsieur Mokati, it is nearly unbelievable how you have changed from an immigrant with bad teeth to a man emanating self-confidence and self-assurance." His words surprised me and made me acutely realize the passage of time, and the inner changes that I must have undergone. Who would I have become without distancing myself from Europe and France? What would I have been like if I had not carried in me the cultural ingredient acquired in my French life of the 1980s? Dr. Fredj's words made me see that I had become a hybrid, a liminal creature that was called to something more than a single cultural mold. From the French perspective, I saw how much America has changed me; from the perspective of Berkeley, I saw that the French ingredient was acting in me to the extent that I could not immerse myself uncritically in the American model of success and achievement at the expenses of a higher *truth*. The sobriety and pessimism of French early modern thought pointed to something that superseded personal happiness. Why can I not be content with even more than that *petit peu* that I had wanted to receive?

Tasso gave me a hint of understanding in regard to my dissatisfaction. When Armida is abandoned by her lover Rinaldo, who is brought to reason by two companions who place his shield in front of him so that he could see his unmanly reflection in it, the poet comments "Il Cielo avaro invidiò il conforto a i tuoi martiri"[29] [a miserly Heaven begrudged you comfort in your sufferings].[30] The notion of *il Cielo avaro* begrudging the sense of fulfillment by reclaiming its part in my happiness, resonated powerfully within me. In that moment when I had all the reasons necessary to be happy and fulfilled, I could not feel it. On the contrary, the better my material situation became, the more miserable I felt. The inner misery I experienced can be only grasped on a spiritual level. I felt absorbed by a mysterious presence that attracted me with an irresistible force, and when I resisted it, it caused torment, comparable only to the loss of a close human being such as a relative or a spouse.

One night, while plunged into deep darkness, I decided to go online and type in the word "Jesuits." I wrote to a vocation contact, who replied to me immediately and we arranged for a meeting in Berkeley. To my amazement, I discovered that there was a contingent of Jesuits living in North Berkeley, studying at the Jesuit School of Theology, part of the Graduate Theological Union. I was appointed a spiritual director, a Jesuit studying to become a priest, who guided me spiritually for about two years until I entered the Jesuit novitiate of the California Province in Culver City.

While discerning my possible vocation, I was completing my dissertation, and one of Corneille's heroes helped pave a path to the religious order. Following *Horace*, I studied *Polyeucte*, that represents an intriguing religious quest, which, on the one hand seeks an answer to the question of "qui nous sommes" [Christian identity], on the other hand, tries to define the relationship between religion and political power.[31] *Polyeucte* relates the rise of Christianity in Roman Armenia during the time of Emperor Decius (250 AD). The title character is an Armenian nobleman married to Pauline, the daughter of Roman Governor Félix. Pauline had been in love with a Roman soldier, Sévère, who is believed to have been killed on the battlefield. Félix did not want Pauline to marry Sévère, given his low birth status. At the inception of the play, Pauline tells her premonitory dream in which she saw Sévère come to Armenia, and then kill her husband. In fact, Sévère is alive and wants to see Pauline. He is no longer a simple soldier, but the emperor's favorite, thanks to his accomplishments on the battlefield. The news of Pauline's marriage shakes his courage. In the meantime, Polyeucte, in an outburst of religious fervor, destroys statues of Roman deities, during a ceremony of sacrifice in the temple. He and his friend, Néarque, are seized by Roman guards and imprisoned. Félix wants to save Polyeucte's life, but the zealous Christian chooses to die. He is executed, and his death brings about Pauline and Félix's conversion to Christianity. Sévère, who witnesses the events, expresses admiration for the Christian faith.

When Polyeucte exhorts his friend, Néarque, to destroy the Roman deities which he considers to be idols ("Allons mon cher Néarque, allons aux yeux des hommes / braver l'idolâtrie, et montrer qui nous sommes"[32] [Come, dear Nearchus, come, in all men's sight / Brave the idolatrous, show what we are][33]), Néarque attempts to temper his friend's eagerness "Ce zèle est trop ardent, souffrez qu'il se modère"[34] [Your zeal is too rush, temper it a little][35]). As the scene between the two friends unfolds, Polyeucte's heroic enthusiasm contaminates Néarque. He repents his moment of weakness:

> Vous sortez du baptême, et ce qui vous anime,
> C'est sa grâce qu'en vous n'affaiblit aucun crime.
> Comme encore tout entière, elle agit pleinement,
> Et tout semble possible à son feu véhément,
> Mais cette même grâce, en moi diminuée,
> et par mille péchés sans cesse exténuée,
> Agit aux grands effets avec tant de langueur
> Que tout semble impossible à son peu de vigueur.
> Cette indigne mollesse et ses lâches défenses
> Sont des punitions qu'attirent mes offenses.
> Mais Dieu, dont on ne doit jamais se défier,
> Me donne votre exemple pour me fortifier.[36]

> [You've been just baptized; what it is spurring you
> Is Heaven's grace, no sin has compromised;
> Still in full spate it sweeps restraints away,
> And all seems possible to its high flood;
> But this some grace, diminished in my soul
> And ever weakened by a thousands of sins,
> Is so enfeebled in its efficacy
> That everything appears beyond its strengths.
> This craven sloth, these cowardly prohibitions
> Are punishments my sins have brought on me;
> But God, on whom we ever should rely,
> Gives me your leadership to strengthen me.][37]

I could relate to Néarque's feeling of shame, as I dragged my life through the meanders of illusions, with too many compromises weakening the overpowering *light of grace*. My sinfulness separated me from the *light of the truth*. Uncomfortable with ideologies of the day, I wandered in darkness, entering the interior of cultures through their languages, hoping to see the way to fulfillment. My native Polish was associated with my troubled childhood. French led me out of hopelessness, but called for discipline and perseverance that I was not ready to embrace. Spanish briefly opened the way to mystery, and Italian to delight. English supplanted Polish in a functional way. But, French never left me. Stubbornly, it pointed to the necessary difficulty of living while standing by an ideal. The plurality of my experience led me to realize that perfection lay beyond the human scope and that the ideal did not lie overseas; it lay beyond the human horizon, and yet, it was reachable by self-emptying and turning one's gaze toward one's heart, in humility and discipline. Hearing Néarque's exhortation that repeats stylistically the verse uttered by Polyeucte, "Allons mon cher Polyeucte, allons aux yeux des hommes / braver l'idolâtrie, et montrer qui nous sommes"[38] I decided to brave the idolatry of secular higher education and to pursue the ideal that, through spiritual direction, manifested itself ever more real. Immediately after earning my PhD, I entered the Society of Jesus.

Chapter Nine

A Coda

The Idiom of the Human Heart

> Pursue love, yet desire earnestly spiritual gifts, but especially that you may prophesy. For one who speaks in a tongue does not speak to men but to God; for no one understands, but in his spirit he speaks mysteries. But one who prophesies speaks to men for edification and exhortation and consolation. One who speaks in a tongue edifies himself; but one who prophesies edifies the church. Now I wish that you all spoke in tongues, but even more that you would prophesy; and greater is one who prophesies than one who speaks in tongues, unless he interprets, so that the church may receive edifying.
> —1 Corinthians 14:1-5 [1]

I am sitting in a restaurant in Oakland with Mathilda Mendelson, whom I have known since my time at San Francisco State University. Our friendship really took off after she learned that I had entered the Jesuit novitiate in Culver City. She attempted to get in touch with me at the beginning of the academic year only to find out from the French department at UC Berkeley that I had become a monk. I remember receiving her e-mail in the novitiate, asking for some explanation about what had happened. Having clarified that my choice to enter religious life was not a result of a trauma, but rather a discerned decision, Mathilda became a faithful supporter of my religious commitment. Our friendship was marked by Mathilda's presence at my Jesuit First Vows ceremony, held after two years as a novitiate, and a decade later, at my priestly ordination, Final Vows in the Society of Jesus. I look with admiration at the witness to the Catholic faith that Mathilda represents. The seed of the Word of God has found a fertile ground in her, as it has remained alive despite storms of secularizing cultural fashion and college peer pressure. The academic environment and her family life, which on the surface did not reverberate anything Catholic, have scratched the surface of the faith but have not uprooted the Word's sprout. I suspect my own decision to give the priority to the spiritual, over a secular career, resonated with Mathilda's inner spiritual tension and watered the exhausted grain of the faith that sought light among the weeds of suffocating ideologies.

Today we don't talk about ideologies, but rather enjoy our Californian dish. Each encounter is a sharing of our underlying enthusiasm for life. Mathilda is a happy mother and wife, though, wrestling with the question why life is so much more elusive and complicated than it needs to be. Her sensitivity for the world's inadequacies, injustices, and mysteries restlessly entertains her clear logical mind, that she employs generously, to the benefit of students in her work as a writing instructor. She is a loving Mary of Magdala figure, wanting Christ to be *where* she passionately expects to find him. As the mystery of Christ's love eludes her feminine expectation, she suffers as a mother, wife, and friend. Yet, she never gives up her remnants of hope generated deeply within her *believing self*. Mathilda has helped me sustain my spiritual growth, like a mirror in which my advancement in the Jesuit life has reflected itself through her responsive, compassionate smiles of approval. She has been a handmaid of the audacious God who called me out of the secular path, into his explicitly clerical service. I am a priest, with nothing of my own. My status is fully unearned by my human effort, but granted freely in a most unexpected fashion, through Berkeley, the enchanted island that has never ceased to appeal to my occasional outbursts of vanity.

The dinner is done; the restaurant owner is giving polite cues to the guests that they should check out. Energized and inspired by the dinner conversation with Mathilda, driving back to San Francisco, I ask myself, "Would I have the same certitude of faith if I had not lived in multiple languages and cultures all these years?" I am not Thérèse of Lisieux who, in a very short life span, had a grasp of the *truth*. I find myself more on the side of the doubting apostle Thomas who needed to see and to touch, to believe. I had to see through illusions constructed by cultures that were inspired by incorrigible pride in their attempts to make humans self-sufficient without God. Earthquakes, storms, fires, and floods have not been enough to break the human pride that keeps reclaiming all that is good in this world for the account of its own enterprise and craft. Through my own pride, I plunged into the vanity of the world through vain loves—pernicious attachments with their ephemeral joys that ultimately generated more hunger than satisfaction.

The experience was painful sometimes, and other times, beautiful, but always unfulfilling. The seeds that the Creator has planted in me, faith, hope, and charity had sprouted but were choked by the weeds of politics, human passion, and other contingencies. I worked my way to become versed in the idioms of diverse cultures which led me to see through the universal human errance. Before returning to the faith in a radical, committed way, I flirted with languages and cultures, not only to ensure my survival, but also to find the answer key to the purpose of the world's busyness.

Living through the gloom of Eastern Europe before the fall of the Iron Curtain in 1989, I rebelled against the political system's attempts to reduce my basic human rights to a desperate animality of survival. I wanted to have the same privileges as the citizens of the opulent capitalist world did: material, political, and spiritual freedom. I discovered, however, that my view of the prosperity of the West was falsified by a lack of direct contact with the reality on the other side of the Iron Curtain. To my surprise, I found out that the freedom of the developed democracies had a high social and psychological cost. The cultures of Western capitalism encouraged the quest for individualistic self-exploration. They let individuals wrestle with the excess of freedom that often led to diverse forms of depression, addiction, and search of artifices in an attempt to anchor that lonely freedom near a comforting shore. Paradoxically, an outgrowth of limitless freedom might be the phenomenon of political correctness. It comes across as a parody of the legal system that should otherwise attempt to protect individual rights.

The chance to have known by experience both sides of the Iron Curtain has given me a skeptical perspective on world cultures. In my skepticism, I take great comfort from the findings of Deconstruction thinkers. Jacques Derrida's critique of logocentrism sheds light on human effort to fix the meaning by imposing an arbitrary correspondence between words and the reality they seek to denote.[2] I find that cultures are tapestries woven from threads of words that first seek to denote reality but soon connote, because words fail to describe our world unequivocally and to explain why we do what we do. They unwittingly displace the meaning, first because of the language's built-in lack of precision. Then, when language users discover that the lack of precision has the creative power of deception, they construct out of words canvases of logical or less logical deformations of the truth, colored by political ideologies in vogue that reward this rhetoric for its service to their interests. The artifice of Western socio-political construct has its roots in *pride*, giving rise to a heroic mode of conduct: the ethos of conquest and empire. On the opposite end of the spectrum, those subjugated to imperialist ideologies respond with a reversed construct of fatalistic victimhood, marked by resentment mixed with self-loathing and megalomania.

Languages are faithful witnesses to human attempts to cope with the vicissitudes of the human condition. They both reflect and inform our perception of the world. In their impossibility to represent the reality, languages project the image of the world as our ideological approximation of the reality in which we sacrifice the truth for comfortable pretense. French grammar, with its early modern neoclassical claims to immutability of form, was a powerful tool of the cultural conquest of Europe that carried with it, its form of life— Frenchness. The success of French at European courts was a victory of "paraître" [make believe], a style that commanded admiration and respect. It ascertained a personal valor of the subject who adhered to and mastered the forms and meanings of the social conduct encoded in and carried within French. It allowed the self-valorization of the subject by providing a framework for negotiating one's path within society.

Nevertheless, contrary to the American penchant for unrestricted personal development, the self-reflectivity dear to French culture keeps in check the excess of individualistic drive for success at the expense of the collectivity. This restraint might have come from residual Catholicism or from its partly Mediterranean heritage, both impregnated with the tragic sense of human predicament. These two ingredients might favor the communal values, while inhibiting the expansion of ego, in a way unknown to the Anglo-Saxon world.

This is perhaps the reason why the French model began to wane when confronted with the new rhetorical forms of self-representation emerging with Anglo-Americanism. The American model has valorized the "I" by subordinating the communal values to its rights. This is reflected in the academic rhetorical model that favors personal claims over other considerations. While the classical model of thesis, antithesis, and synthesis has been favored by the French tradition that presented it to itself, and to the world, as a universal model of reasoning, the American rhetorical model has progressively opted, it seems, for thesis as the most important element of an essay. The truth has been less an outcome of the social consensus, the fruit of a dialectical process; rather the "I" could marshal, by supporting his or her personal claim, the argument that would serve the "I's" self-interest. Surely, the approach makes life easier for the subject who does not need to pay homage to a tradition: one can challenge it with a clever, seductive argument that the populace might like, and even applaud. In my case, being able to ascertain the rights to my subjectivity in the academic setting was instrumental for me in succeeding in the academic venture in the United States.

Yet I remain fully aware that there is a whole world, a whole cultural territory, now much more expansive than what is usually referred to as the first world, where the subject's "I" has less freedom. Intimidated and surrendered to one's cultural framework, the "I" reproduces the model of the authority not only accepted but also uncontested for centuries. In many cultures, there is no point in arguing for the progress of ideas because the world is as it is. Cultures marked by Eastern religions would affirm that truth. This is why some Asian students who want to study the humanities in the West find it difficult to overcome the otherness of their way of seeing the world.

There you have our world of logical argument, a rational world of progress, the linear emancipation of the *self* from the communal constraints of tradition. There must be another way of living, another purpose for our being on Earth, than merely arguing on the political plane. There must be another reality that lies beyond greed, self-absorption, and a maniacal drive for control of the other. It lies, unfortunately, beyond the thick screen of delusion, woven by cultures that fearfully and forcefully hide another possibility of living. This other form of life[3] is available to us when we reach the point of being able to remove the curtain of illusion, and the wall of deceit. Good literature offers us hints, and even guidance, of how to undertake the struggle against the lack of authenticity in our lives. I have been fortunate to be exposed to those works. The freedom of approaches in the American system led to a greater appreciation of the works of European masters. That freedom created, at the same time, the need to bound it by a system of beliefs that would limit the danger of egocentric self-expansion.

Who would I have become if I had not spent nearly a decade in France learning rudiments of various jobs? What would have become of me if I had not had that first contact with a Jesuit school at Saint Louis de Gonzague? What would have happened if I had not continued studying French literature at UC Berkeley and instead had chosen a different path? Pulling me back from the enchantment of American individualism present in my everyday life, the French way of the Grand Siècle, that is the seventeenth century, with its moderation and skepticism led me to the truth. While reading its authors, whose thoughts and attitudes were frequently formed by Jesuit pedagogy, I learned skepticism and caution. These authors' philosophies and ideals made me rethink what I had gained in my challenging twenties spent on French soil. Ultimately, the French skill for interiority and self-reflectivity redirected me to the foundations of my faith, dissipated by the worldly adventure. It made me rediscover the way of Jesus of Nazareth. I suddenly felt in me the imprint of the old Christian truth: Jesus did what is to be experienced by all human beings—be born, suffer among small joys, die, be buried, and eventually resurrected. I know from experience about all the stages, except the final, the glorious one that I must accept by faith. If I refuse to believe, I shall fall prey to the circle of absurdity in our world.

Likely Western epic canvasses (epitomized prominently in this century by the great American empire) that depict ideologies of conquest in their enlightened foundations of pride, have the destiny of the Tower of Babel that crumbled under the weight of its unchecked size. I believe that nationalisms and imperialisms, by cultivating in them the foundational seed of *amourpropre* inherited from Adam's transgression, obfuscate the fundamental truth of the purpose of human existence that Jesus Christ has exemplified. National cultures and languages camouflage, in their core, the simplicity of Christ's message: life is beautiful in its fragility but not when it attempts to impress with the unleashed human spirit of independence and self-aggrandizement. That spirit ineluctably turns into the oppressor of the other. To be effective, it rallies the critical mass, like it did during the Bolshevik Revolution in Russia in 1917 ("Bolshevick" coming from the word "majority"). Under oppression of that majority, the folk must sever or absorb the symbolism of the supernatural for their own gain so that they will no longer aspire to anything else but *the petit peu* for survival. Little by little, the folk will become subservient to the great mogul, a merchant of ideologically controlled dreams and aspirations of which they become slaves. The mogul creates a curtain, a screen that he jealously keeps before the eyes of the deceived so that they can see only that which serve the ideology of surrender and subservience. Yes, cultures and languages are the mogul's social tools: they have been cultivated by generations to mold the behaviors, reactions, and emotions of their users. Yet as dynamic entities, they can also help emancipate one from the dominant mold by opening the way to spirituality—the domain that lies above the language, and above the culture, but uses it as its springboard.

Jesuit spirituality, without denying anything from daily reality, offers and provides a bridge between the experience of the ordinary and the supernatural. The supernatural is not a frivolous fruit of the imagination; it is as real as water. It is a paradox of our civilization that it has adopted as its objective, a so-called scientific mission for the betterment of the world. Without denying the good use of empiricism for our daily life, there is no need to dismiss the spiritual contemplative domain.

In Jesuit spirituality, one starts contemplating the incarnate reality by listening to it patiently, until it *speaks* to the beholder. A meditation of a biblical scene in which the incarnate God acts and speaks establishes such a connection between the human world and the divine, between the subjectivity of the beholder and the objectivity of the mystery that enters, through the exercise, the interiority of the one who seeks. This revelation released me from the burden of the experience of multilingualism and multiculturalism. It has established belief as the only reality that matters. Languages and cultures in their diversity are scaffolding that lead me to reach the elusive Heaven—where difference dies, giving life to universal rejoicing in angelic harmony. I am on the journey. Would I have traded it for another road? Possibly, but would I have come out with the same gain? I would have gained that *petit peu* of the common bourgeois but unlikely the vision that allows a glimpse into the *mystery*.

Notes

PROLOGUE

1. Benedict XVI, "Homily of His Holiness Pope Benedict XVI: Solemnity of the Sacred Heart of Jesus," transcript of mass, St. Peter's Square (June 11, 2010), http://www.vatican.va/holy_father/benedict_xvi/homilies/2010/documents/hf_ben-xvi_hom_20100611_concl-anno-sac_en.html (accessed May 2, 2016).

1. WHEN LIFE WAS A FRENCH DREAM

1. Quotations and translations from François Villon are from *The Poems of François Villon*, ed. Galway Kinnell, New ed. (London and Hanover, NH: University Press of New England, 1982).
2. Villon, "Ballade des dames du temps jadis," in *Poems*, 46.
3. Villon, "Ballade des dames du temps jadis," in *Poems*, 47.
4. Anne Applebaum's book, *Iron Curtain: The Crushing of Eastern Europe 1944-1956* (Toronto and New York: Doubleday, 2012), is an excellent study of the onset of totalitarianism in Central Europe.
5. The "Marshall Plan," formally U.S. Congress, *European Cooperation Act of 1948*, Public Law 80-472, 80th Cong., 2nd sess. (April 3, 1948): 137-59.
6. On the value of truth and sincerity in verbal interaction in Polish, see Anna Wierzbicka's section "'Tact' and 'Sincerity'" in her article "Two languages, two cultures, one (?) self: Between Polish and English," in *Translating Lives: Living with Two Languages and Cultures*, ed. Mary Besemeres and Anna Wierzbicka (St Lucia: University of Queensland Press, 2007), 104.
7. Jean Cocteau and Jeanne-Marie Leprince de Beaumont, *La belle et la bête*, directed by Jean Cocteau (France: DisCina, 1946).

2. OUTPOURING OF THE DREAM INTO REAL LIFE

1. André Lagarde and Laurent Michard, *Collection littéraire Lagarde et Michard* (Paris: Bordas, 1982; first published 1948), in 6 vols.
2. The Oxford text in *The Song of Roland*, ed. Gerard J. Brault (London and University Park: Pennsylvania State University Press, 1978), 66, vv. 1049-54.
3. *The Song of Roland: Translations of the Versions in Assonance and Rhyme of the "Chanson de Roland,"* trans. Joseph J. Duggan and Annalee C. Rejhon (Turnhout, Belgium: Brepols, 2012), 66.
4. François Villon, "La ballade des pendus," in *The Poems of François Villon*, trans. Galway Kinnell, New ed. (London and Hanover, NH: University Press of New England, 1982), 208.
5. François Villon, "La ballade des pendus," in *The Poems of François Villon*, trans. Galway Kinnell, New ed. (London and Hanover, NH: University Press of New England, 1982), 209.
6. Jean Racine, *Andromaque*, act 4, scene 1, in *Oeuvres complètes*, ed. Raymond Picard. Bibliothèque de la Pléiade (Paris: Gallimard, 1960), 283.
7. Jean Racine, *Andromaque*, act 4, scene 1, trans. A. S. Kline, http://www.poetryintranslation.com/PITBR/French/Andromache.htm (accessed September 9, 2013).
8. Gérard de Nerval, *Les filles du feu*, in *Oeuvres*, ed. Jean Richer. Bibliothèque de la Pléiade (Paris: Gallimard, 1960), 147-344.
9. Gérard de Nerval, *The Chimeras*, trans. Peter Jay (Redding Ridge, CT: Black Swan Books, 1984), 14-15.
10. "Warsaw Pact," "Treaty of Friendship, Co-operation, and Mutual Assistance..." May 14, 1955, *North Atlantic Treaty Organization* (NATO), http://avalon.law.yale.edu/20th_century/warsaw.asp (accessed May 15, 2016).

3. THE DREAM BECOMING FLESH

1. Claire J. Kramsch, *The Multilingual Subject: What Foreign Language Learners Say About Their Experience and Why It Matters* (Oxford: Oxford University Press, 2009), 6.
2. Albert Camus, *L'Étranger* (Paris: Gallimard, 1942); André Gide, *Les Caves du Vatican* (Paris: Nouvelle Revue Française, 1914).
3. The Prefecture of Paris is a French administration department that is part of the Ministry of the Interior, which is responsible for issuing documents, such as identity cards, passports, and permits for foreigners, as well as responsibility for the management of the police and firefighters.
4. Dante Alighieri, *Divine Comedy*, written c. 1308-1320, originally titled *Comedìa*. The poem was first published as *Divina Comedia* (Vinegia, Italy: Gabriele Giolito de' Ferrari, 1555).

4. ROLLING IN THE DEEP

1. Gustave Flaubert, *Bouvard et Pécuchet: Oeuvre posthume* (Paris: Garnier Frères, 1965).
2. Claire J. Kramsch, *The Multilingual Subject: What Foreign Language Learners Say About Their Experience and Why It Matters* (Oxford: Oxford University Press, 2009), 96-98.
3. Julia Kristeva, *Revolution in Poetic Language*, trans. Margaret Waller (New York: Columbia University Press, 1984; first published in French in 1974).

4. Kramsch, *Multilingual Subject*, 96-98.
5. Flaubert, *Bouvard et Pécuchet*, 190.
6. Gustave Flaubert, *Bouvard and Récuchet: A Tragic-Comic Novel of Bourgeois life*, trans. Walter Dunne (Chicago: Simon P. Magee, 1904), 370, https://www.gutenberg.org/files/25014/25014-h/25014-h.htm (accessed July 5, 2016).
7. Henri Michaux, "La Parpue," in *La nuit remue* (Paris: Gallimard, 1935), http://www.etudes-litteraires.com/forum/topic18702-henri-michaux-la-nuit-remue-la-parpue.html (accessed July 7, 2016).
8. Molière's plays in order of performance: *Tartuffe* (1664), *Dom Juan* (1665), *Le Misanthrope* (1666); and Pierre Choderlos de Laclos, *Les Liaisons dangereuses* (Amsterdam: Durand, 1782).
9. Molière, *Le Misanthrope*, in *Oeuvres completes*, ed. Maurice Rat, vol. 2, Bibliothèque de la Pléiade. (Paris: Gallimard, 1956) act 1, scene 1, 44.
10. Molière, *Le Misanthrope*, trans. Henri Van Laun, act 1, scene 1, 89-96, https://ebooks.adelaide.edu.au/m/moliere/misanthrope/act1.html (accessed May 13, 2016).
11. Henri Michaux, "Ma vie," in *La Nuit remue*, http://www.poesie.net/michaux1.htm (accessed July 7, 2016).
12. Henri Michaux, "Ma vie," in *La Nuit remue*, trans. Valerie Smith and James Bushnik, http://www.reelyredd.com/0605.michaux_ma_vie.htm (accessed May 13, 2016).
13. Adele and Paul Epworth, "Rolling in the Deep," November 29, 2010, digital compact disc (London: Eastcote Studios, 2010).
14. Blaise Pascal (1623-1662) was a seventeenth-century French philosopher, mathematician, and physicist. His notes on religious philosophy were published posthumously in *Pensées de m. Pascal sur la religion et sur quelques autres sujets* , ed. Etienne Périer and Florin Périer (A Paris: Chez Guillaume Desprez, 1670).
15. Matthew 18:3, http://www.biblica.com/en-us/bible/online-bible/nasb/matthew/18/.
16. Fyodor Dostoyevsky, *The Eternal Husband*, trans. Max Bollinger (London: Sovereign, 2012). First published in 1870 in *Zarya Magazine*, Saint Petersburg.
17. Georges Bernanos, *The Diary of a Country Priest*, trans. Pamela Morris (New York: Macmillan, 1937). First published as *Journal d'un curé de campagne* (Paris: Plon, 1936).
18. Paul Claudel, *L'Annonce faite à Marie*, vol. 2 of *Théâtre de Paul Claudel*, ed. Jacques Madaule, Bibliothèque de la Pléiade (Paris: Gallimard, 1956), 130-215; 1st version published in 1912.

5. SAINT LOUIS DE GONZAGUE: FORESHADOWING

1. John S. Ambler offers a thorough analysis of Alain Savary's reform in chap. 7, "Constraints on Policy Innovation in Education: Thatcher's Britain and Mitterrand's France," in *Education in France: Continuity and Change in the Mitterrand Years, 1981-1995*, ed. Anne Corbett and Bob Moon (New York: Routledge, 1996), 93-118.
2. Ernest Hemingway, *The Sun Also Rises* (New York: Charles Scribner, 1926).
3. Patricia Highsmith and Wim Wenders, *Der amerikanische Freund* [*The American Friend*], directed by Wim Wenders (West Germany and France: Axiom Films, 1977), adapted from Highsmith's novel, *Ripley's Game* (London: Heinemann; and New York: Random House,1974).
4. Simone Weil, *La Pesanteur et la grâce* (Paris: Plon, 1943).

6. SAN FRANCISCO

1. Stephen Krashen, *The Input Hypothesis: Issues and Implications* (New York: Longman, 1985).

2. Patricia Highsmith and Wim Wenders, *Der amerikanische Freund* [*The American Friend*], directed by Wim Wenders (West Germany and France: Axiom Films, 1977).

3. Jaufré [Joffré] Rudel, "Lanquan li jorn son lonc en mai," in *The Songs of Jaufré Rudel*, ed. and trans. Rupert T. Pickens (Toronto: Pontifical Institute of Medieval Studies, 1978), 170, lines 1-4.

4. Rudel, "Lanquan li jorn son lonc en mai," 171.

5. Plato, *Phaedrus* (c. 370 BC), the translations by Benjamin Jowett is available online at http://www.gutenberg.org/ebooks/1636 (accessed May 14, 2016); Giovanni Pico della Mirandola, *Oration on the Dignity of Man*, trans. A. Robert Caponigri (Washington, DC: Regnery Gateway, 1956); Meister Eckhart, *The Essential Sermons, Commentaries, Treatises and Defense*, ed. and trans. Bernard McGinn and Edmund Colledge (New York: Paulist Press, 1981).

6. Elvis Presley, "Lonesome Cowboy," *Loving You*, July 1, 1957, RCA Victor, The song was written by Sid Tepper and Roy C. Bennett.

7. François Rabelais, *La vie de Gargantua et de Pantagruel* [*The Life of Gargantua and of Pantagruel*] (c. 1532-1564), in *Five Books of the Lives, Heroic Deeds and Sayings of Gargantua and his Son Pantagruel. The Works of Rabelais*, trans. Thomas Urquhart and Peter Antony Motteux (Derby, UK: Moray Press, 1894), https://www.gutenberg.org/files/1200/1200-h/1200-h.htm (accessed May 15, 2016).

8. Michel de Montaigne, "Au Lecteur," in *Oeuvres comlpètes de Montaigne*, ed. Albert Thibaudet and Maurice Rat, Vol. 2. Bibliothèque de la Pléiade (Paris: Gallimard, 1962); "To the Reader," In *The Essays of Michel de Montaigne*, trans. M. A. Screech (London: Allen Lane, Penguin Press, 1991), lvix.

9. Montaigne, "Of Liberty of Conscience," in *Essays*, 763.

10. Denis Diderot, *Les Bijoux indiscrets* (Monomotapa [i. e. Paris]: n.p., [c. 1748]).

11. Gabriel García Márquez, *One Hundred Years of Solitude*, trans. Gregory Rabassa (New York: Harper & Row, 1970).

12. Pedro Calderón de la Barca, *La vida es sueño* (Madrid: Cátedra, 1991), 165, line 2187.

7. O BEAUTIFUL!

1. Charles Baudelaire, "L'Invitation au voyage," in *Baudelaire: Œuvres, Le Speen de Paris*, ed. Y.-G. Le Dantec, Bibliothèque de la Pléiade (Paris: Gallimard, 1931), vol. 1, 431.

2. Charles Baudelaire, *The Poems and Prose Poems of Charles Baudelaire*, ed. James Huneker (New York: Brentano, 1919), http://www.gutenberg.org/files/36287/36287-h/36287-h.htm (accessed May 15, 2016).

3. Jan Potocki and Tadeusz Kwiatkowski, *Saragossa Manuscript*, directed by Wojciech Has, Poland: Kamera Films, 1965.

4. Matthew 25:30, *New American Standard Bible*, http://www.biblica.com/en-us/bible/online-bible/nasb/matthew/25/ (accessed July 10, 2016).

5. Isidore of Seville, *Etymologiae* [*Etymologies*](c. 600-625), trans. Stephen A. Barney and others (Cambridge: Cambridge University Press, 2006).

6. The "Warsaw Pact," formally "Treaty of Friendship, Co-operation, and Mutual Assistance..." May 14, 1955, *North Atlantic Treaty Organization* (NATO), http://avalon.law.yale.edu/20th_century/warsaw.asp (accessed May 15, 2016).

7. Maria Dąbrowska, *Noce i dnie* [*Nights and Days*] (Warszawa: Mortkowicz, 1932-1934).

8. *The Song of Roland: Translations of the Versions in Assonance and Rhyme of the "Chanson de Roland*," trans. Joseph J. Duggan and Annalee C. Rejhon (Turnhout, Belgium: Brepols, 2012).

9. Joseph J. Duggan, *The "Cantar de mio Cid": Poetic Creation in Its Economic and Social Contexts* (New York: Cambridge University Press, 1989).

10. Jaufré [Joffré] Rudel, "Lanquan li jorn son lonc en mai," in *The Songs of Jaufré Rudel*, ed. and trans. Rupert T. Pickens (Toronto: Pontifical Institute of Medieval Studies, 1978).

11. William IX, Duke of Aquitaine [Guilhen de Peitieu], "Farai un vers pos mi sonelh" ["The Ladies with the Cat"]," in *Lark in the Morning: The Verses of the Troubadours. A*

Bilingual Edition, ed. Robert Kehew, trans. Ezra Pound et al. (Chicago: University of Chicago Press, 2005), 28-33.
  12. William IX, "Farai un vers pos mi sonelh."
  13. Petrarch, *The Canzoniere or Rerum vulgarium fragmenta*, ed. and trans. Mark Musa (Bloomington: Indiana University Press, 1996).
  14. Petrarch, "Letter to Posterity," in *Petrarch: The First Modern Scholar and Man of Letters*, ed. and trans. James Harvey Robinson (New York: G. P. Putnam, 1898), 61.

8. FROM ILLUSION TO THE TRUTH

  1. François Rabelais, *The Life of Gargantua and of Pantagruel* (c. 1532-1564), in *Five Books of the Lives, Heroic Deeds and Sayings of Gargantua and his Son Pantagruel. The Works of Rabelais. The Works of Rabelais*, trans. Thomas Urquhart and Peter Antony Motteux (Derby, UK: Moray Press, 1894), https://www.gutenberg.org/files/1200/1200-h/1200-h.htm (accessed May 15, 2016).
  2. Edwin Duval, *The Design of Rabelais's Pantagruel* (New Haven, CT: Yale University Press, 1991).
  3. Terence Cave, *The Cornucopian Text: Problems of Writing in the French Renaissance* (New York and Oxford: Oxford University Press, 1979); Mikhail Bakhtin, *Rabelais and His World*, trans. Hélène Iswolsky (Bloomington : Indiana University Press, 1968).
  4. Sacha Baron Cohen, Anthony Hines, and others, *Borat: Cultural Learnings of America for Make Benefit Glorious Nation of Kazakhstan*, directed by Larry Charles (Los Angeles: Four By Two Films, 20th Century Fox, 2006).
  5. Torquato Tasso, *Gerusalemme liberata* (1581), 2nd ed., ed. Bruno Maier (Milano: Rizzoli, 1988).
  6. Aristotle, *Poetics* (c. 335 BCE), trans. Gerard F. Else (1970; Ann Arbor: University of Michigan Press, 1990).
  7. Pierre Corneille, *Le Cid*, in *Oeuvres complètes*, ed. André Stegmann (Paris: Seuil, 1963), 215-41.
  8. Marc Fumaroli, *Héros et orateurs* (Geneva: Droz, 1996).
  9. Tasso, *Gerusalemme liberata*; and Ludovico Ariosto, *Orlando furioso* (1516; 1532), trans. Guido Waldman (Oxford: Oxford University Press, 1998).
  10. On Tasso's reception in France in the early seventeenth century, see A. Donald Sellstrom, *Corneille, Tasso and Modern Poetics* (Columbus: Ohio State University Press, 1986), 3-16; Lawrence F. Rhu, *The Genesis of Tasso's Narrative Theory* (Detroit: Wayne State University Press, 1993).
  11. John Schulian and others, *Xena: Warrior Princess* (Auckland, New Zealand: MCA Television, Renaissance Pictures, 1995-2001).
  12. On New Historicism as a critical tool, see Lois Tyson, *Critical Theory Today: A User-Friendly Guide*, 2nd ed. (New York: Routledge, 2006), in particular 278-300.
  13. Torquato Tasso, *Aminta* (Vinegia, Italy: [Aldus], 1581); and *Discorsi dell'arte poetica* (Venetia, Italy: Ad instanza di Giulio Vassalini, 1587); Tasso, *Gerusalemme liberata*.
  14. Tasso, *Gerusalemme liberata*, canto 1, stanza 2.
  15. Torquato Tasso, *Jerusalem Delivered: An English Prose Version*, trans. Ralph Nash (Detroit: Wayne State University Press, 1987), 470.
  16. Tasso, *Jerusalem Delivered*, 471.
  17. On the conflict between virtue and idleness in Tasso, see Brian Vickers, "Leisure and Idleness in the Renaissance: The Ambivalence of Otium," *Renaissance Studies* 4, no. 2 (1990): 135-36.
  18. Tasso, *Gerusalemme liberata*, canto 4, stanza 33.
  19. Tasso, *Jerusalem Delivered*, 75.
  20. Plato, *Republic* (c. 380 BC), trans. Benjamin Jowett, https://www.gutenberg.org/ebooks/1497 (accessed May 16, 2016).
  21. Simone Weil, *La Pesanteur et la grâce* (Paris: Plon, 1943).

22. Pierre Corneille, *Horace*, in *Oeuvres complètes*, ed. André Stegmann (Paris: Seuil, 1963), act 2, scene 3, lines 491-94.
23. Translations for Pierre Corneille's plays are from *Seven Plays*, trans. Samuel Solomon (New York: Random House, 1969), 142.
24. Simone Weil, *The Need for Roots: Prelude to a Declaration of Duties Toward Mankind* (London: Routledge & Kegan Paul, 1952), 136.
25. Corneille, *Horace*, in *Oeuvres complètes*, act 5, scene 3, lines 1753-58.
26. Corneille, *Horatius*, in *Seven Plays*, trans. Solomon, 187-88.
27. Corneille, *Le Cid*, in *Oeuvres completes*, act 2, scene 6, lines 595-98.
28. Corneille, *Le Cid*, in *Seven Plays*, trans. Solomon, act 2, scene 6, 595-98.
29. Tasso, *Gerusalemme liberata*, canto 16, stanza 61.
30. Tasso, *Jerusalem Delivered*, trans. Nash, 352.
31. Pierre Corneille, *Polyeucte* (c. 1641-1642) (Paris: A. de Sommaville et A. Courbé, 1643).
32. Corneille, *Polyeucte*, in *Oeuvres complètes*, ed. Stegmann, act 2, scene 6, lines 645-46.
33. Corneille, *Polyeucte*, trans. Solomon, lines act 2, scene 6, 645-46.
34. Corneille, *Polyeucte*, act 2, scene 6, lines 653.
35. Corneille, *Polyeucte*, trans. Solomon, act 2, scene 6, lines 653.
36. Corneille, *Polyeucte*, act 2, scene 6, lines 693-704.
37. Corneille, *Polyeucte*, trans. Solomon, act 2, scene 6, lines 693-704.
38. Corneille, *Polyeucte*, act 2, scene 6, lines 705-6.

9. A CODA

1. Corinthians 14:1-5, http://www.biblica.com/en-us/bible/online-bible/nasb/1-corinthians/14/ (accessed July 9, 2016).
2. Jacques Derrida, *Of Grammatology*, trans. by Gayatri Chakravorty Spivak (Baltimore: Johns Hopkins University Press, 1997).
3. J. F. M. Hunter, "'Forms of Life' in Wittgenstein's *Philosophical Investigations*," *American Philosophical Quarterly* 5, no. 4 (October 1968): 233-43, http://www.jstor.org.ignacio.usfca.edu/stable/20009278 (accessed July 11, 2016).

Bibliography

Ambler, John S. "Constraints on Policy Innovation in Education: Thatcher's Britain and Mitterrand's France." In *Education in France: Continuity and Change in the Mitterrand Years, 1981-1995*, edited by Anne Corbett and Bob Moon, 93-118. New York: Routledge, 1996.
Applebaum, Anne. *Iron Curtain: The Crushing of Eastern Europe 1944-1956*. Toronto and New York: Doubleday, 2012.
Ariosto, Ludovico. *Orlando furioso* (1516; 1532). Translated by Guido Waldman. 1974. World's Classics. Oxford: Oxford University Press, 1983.
Aristotle. *Poetics* (c. 335 BCE). Translated by Gerard F. Else. 1970. Ann Arbor Paperbacks. Ann Arbor: University of Michigan Press, 1990.
Bakhtin, Mikhail. *Rabelais and His World*. Translated by Hélène Iswolsky. Bloomington: Indiana University Press, 1968.
Baron Cohen, Sacha, Anthony Hines, Peter Baynham, Dan Mazer, and Todd Phillips. *Borat: Cultural Learnings of America for Make Benefit Glorious Nation of Kazakhstan*. Directed by Larry Charles. Los Angeles: Four By Two Films, 20th Century Fox, 2006.
Baudelaire, Charles. *Œuvres complètes de Charles Baudelaire*. 4 vols. Paris: Michel Lévy frères, 1869.
———. *Baudelaire: Œuvres, Le Speen de Paris*. Edited by Y.-G. Le Dantec. Bibliothèque de la Pléiade (Paris: Gallimard, 1931).
———. *The Poems and Prose Poems of Charles Baudelaire*. Edited by James Huneker. New York: Brentano, 1919. Available online at http://www.gutenberg.org/files/36287/36287-h/36287-h.htm (accessed May 15, 2016).
Benedict XVI. "Homily of His Holiness Pope Benedict XVI: Solemnity of the Sacred Heart of Jesus." Transcript of Mass at St. Peter's Square. June 11, 2010. http://www.vatican.va/holy_father/benedict_xvi/homilies/2010/documents/hf_ben-xvi_hom_20100611_concl-anno-sac_en.html (accessed May 2, 2016).
Bernanos, Georges. *The Diary of a Country Priest*. Translated by Pamela Morris. New York: Macmillan, 1937.
———. *Journal d'un curé de campagne*. Paris: Plon, 1936.
Besemeres, Mary, and Anna Wierzbicka, eds. *Translating Lives: Living with Two Languages and Cultures*. St Lucia: University of Queensland Press, 2007.
Calderón de la Barca, Pedro. *La vida es sueño*. Madrid: Cátedra, 1991.
Camus, Albert. *L'Étranger*. Paris: Gallimard, 1942.
Cave, Terence. *The Cornucopian Text: Problems of Writing in the French Renaissance*. New York and Oxford: Oxford University Press, 1979.
Choderlos de Laclos, Pierre Ambroise François. *Les Liaisons dangereuses*. 4 vols. Amsterdam: Durand, 1782.

Claudel, Paul. *L'Annonce faite à Marie* (1912). Vol. 2 of *Théâtre de Paul Claudel*. Edited by Jacques Madaule, 130-215. Bibliothèque de la Pléiade. Paris: Gallimard, 1956. First published 1912.
Cocteau, Jean, and Jeanne-Marie Leprince de Beaumont. *La belle et la bête*. Directed by Jean Cocteau. France: DisCina, 1946.
Corneille, Pierre. *Le Cid*. In *Oeuvres complètes*. Edited by André Stegmann. Paris: Seuil, 1963.
———. *Horace*. In *Oeuvres complètes*. Edited by André Stegmann. Paris: Seuil, 1963.
———. *Polyeucte*. In *Oeuvres complètes*. Edited by André Stegmann. Paris: Seuil, 1963.
———. *Seven Plays*. Translated by Samuel Solomon. New York: Random House, 1969.
Dąbrowska, Maria. *Noce i dnie*. 4 vols. Warszawa: Mortkowicz, 1932-1934.
Dante Alighieri. *Divina Comedia [Divine Comedy]*. Vinegia, Italy: Gabriele Giolito de' Ferrari, 1555.
Derrida, Jacques. *Of Grammatology*. Translated by Gayatri Chakravorty Spivak. Baltimore: Johns Hopkins University Press, 1997.
Diderot, Denis. *Les Bijoux indiscrets*. Monomotapa [i. e. Paris]: n.p., [c. 1748].
Dostoyevsky, Fyodor. *The Eternal Husband* (1870). Translated by Max Bollinger. London: Sovereign, 2012.
Duggan, Joseph J. *The "Cantar de mio Cid": Poetic Creation in Its Economic and Social Contexts*. New York: Cambridge University Press, 1989.
Duval, Edwin. *The Design of Rabelais's Pantagruel*. New Haven, CT: Yale University Press, 1991.
Eckhart, Meister. *The Essential Sermons, Commentaries, Treatises and Defense*. Edited and translated by Bernard McGinn and Edmund Colledge. New York: Paulist Press, 1981.
Flaubert, Gustave. *Bouvard et Pécuchet: Oeuvre posthume* (1881). Paris: Garnier Frères, 1965.
———. *Bouvard and Récuchet: A Tragic-Comic Novel of Bourgeois life*. Translated by Walter Dunne. Chicago: Simon P. Magee, 1904. Available online at https://www.gutenberg.org/files/25014/25014-h/25014-h.htm (accessed July 5, 2016).
Fumaroli, Marc. *Héros et orateurs*. Geneva: Droz, 1996.
García Marquez, Gabriel. *One Hundred Years of Solitude*. Translation by Gregory Rabassa. New York: Harper & Row, 1970.
Gide, André. *Les Caves du Vatican*. Paris: Nouvelle Revue Française, 1914.
Hampton, Timothy. *Writing from History: The Rhetoric of Exemplarity in Renaissance Literature*. Ithaca, NY: Cornell University Press, 1990.
Hemingway, Ernest. *The Sun Also Rises*. New York: Charles Scribner, 1926.
Highsmith, Patricia. *Ripley's Game*. London: Heinemann; and New York: Random House,1974.
Highsmith, Patricia, and Wim Wenders. *Der amerikanische Freund [The American Friend]*. Directed by Wim Wenders. West Germany and France: Axiom Films, 1977.
Hunter, J. F. M. "'Forms of Life' in Wittgenstein's *Philosophical Investigations*." *American Philosophical Quarterly* 5, no. 4 (October 1968): 233-43. Available online at http://www.jstor.org.ignacio.usfca.edu/stable/20009278 (accessed July 11, 2016).
Isidore of Seville, *Etymologiae [Etymologies]*(c. 600-625). Translated by Stephen A. Barney and others. Cambridge: Cambridge University Press, 2006.
Kramsch, Claire J. *The Multilingual Subject: What Foreign Language Learners Say About Their Experience and Why It Matters*. Oxford: Oxford University Press, 2009.
Krashen, Stephen. *The Input Hypothesis: Issues and Implications*. New York: Longman, 1985.
Kristeva, Julia. *Revolution in Poetic Language*. Translated by Margaret Waller. New York: Columbia University Press, 1984. First published in French 1974.
Lagarde, André, and Laurent Michard. *Collection littéraire Lagarde et Michard*. 6 vols. Paris: Bordas, 1982. First published 1948.
Michaux, Henri. *La nuit remue*. Paris: Gallimard, 1935.
———. "Ma vie." In *La Nuit remue*, translated by Valerie Smith and James Bushnik. Available online at http://www.reelyredd.com/0605.michaux_ma_vie.htm (accessed May 13, 2016).
———. "La Parpue." In *La nuit remue* (Paris: Gallimard, 1935). Available online at http://www.etudes-litteraires.com/forum/topic18702-henri-michaux-la-nuit-remue-la-parpue.html (accessed July 7, 2016).

Molière. *Dom Juan ou le Festin de pierre.* Amsterdam: [Henricus Wetstein], 1683.
———. *Le Misanthrope.* In *Oeuvres complètes.* Edited by Maurice Rat, vol. 2, Bibliothèque de la Pléiade. Paris: Gallimard, 1956.
———. *Le Misanthrope.* Translated by Henri Van Laun. Available online at https://ebooks.adelaide.edu.au/m/moliere/misanthrope/act1.html (accessed May 13, 2016).
Montaigne, Michel de. "Au Lecteur." in *Oeuvres comlpètes de Montaigne.* Edited by Albert Thibaudet and Maurice Rat. Vol. 2. Bibliothèque de la Pléiade. Paris: Gallimard, 1962.
———. "To the Reader." In *The Essays of Michel de Montaigne.* Translated by M. A. Screech, lvix. London: Allen Lane, Penguin Press, 1991.
Motyka, Matthew. "A Historicization of an Ideal: Poetic Practice in the Work of Three Counter Reformation Writers, Torquato Tasso, Pierre Corneille, and Lope de Vega. PhD diss., University of California, Berkeley, 2000.
Nerval, Gérard de. *Oeuvres.* Edited by Jean Richer. 2 vols. Bibliothèque de la Péiade. Paris: Gallimard, 1960.
———. *The Chimeras.* Translated by Peter Jay. Essays by Richard Holmes and Peter Jay. Redding Ridge, CT: Black Swan Books, 1984.
New American Standard Bible. 2002. Available online at http://www.biblica.com/en-us/bible/online-bible/nasb/ (accessed June 15, 2016).
Pascal, Blaise. *Pensées de m. Pascal sur la religion et sur quelques autres sujets.* Edited by Etienne Périer and Florin Périer. A Paris: Chez Guillaume Desprez, 1670.
Petrarch. *The Canzoniere or Rerum vulgarium fragmenta.* Edited and translated by Mark Musa. Bloomington: Indiana University Press, 1996.
———. "Letter to Posterity." In *Petrarch: The First Modern Scholar and Man of Letters.* Edited and translated by James Harvey Robinson, 61. New York: G. P. Putnam, 1898.
Pico della Mirandola, Giovanni. *Oration on the Dignity of Man.* Translated by A. Robert Caponigri. Washington, DC: Regnery Gateway, 1956.
Plato. *Phaedrus* (c. 370 BC). Translation by Benjamin Jowett. Available online at http://www.gutenberg.org/ebooks/1636 (accessed May 14, 2016).
———. *Republic* (c. 380 BC). Translation by Benjamin Jowett. Available online at https://www.gutenberg.org/ebooks/1497 (accessed May 16, 2016).
Potocki, Jan, and Tadeusz Kwiatkowski. *Saragossa Manuscript.* Directed by Wojciech Has. Poland: Kamera Films, 1965.
Rabelais, François. *The Life of Gargantua and of Pantagruel* (c. 1532-1564). In *Five Books of the Lives, Heroic Deeds and Sayings of Gargantua and his Son Pantagruel. The Works of Rabelais. The Works of Rabelais,* translated by Thomas Urquhart and Peter Antony Motteux. Derby, UK: Moray Press, 1894. Available online at https://www.gutenberg.org/files/1200/1200-h/1200-h.htm (accessed May 15, 2016).
Jean Racine, *Andromaque.* In *Oeuvres complètes,* edited by Raymond Picard. Bibliothèque de la Pléiade. Paris: Gallimard, 1960.
Racine, Jean. *Andromaque.* Translated by A. S. Kline. Available online at http://www.poetryintranslation.com/PITBR/French/Andromache.htm (accessed September 9, 2013).
Rhu, Lawrence F. *The Genesis of Tasso's Narrative Theory.* Detroit: Wayne State University Press, 1993.
Robinson, James Harvey, ed. and trans. *Petrarch: The First Modern Scholar and Man of Letters.* New York: G. P. Putnam, 1898.
Rudel, Joffré [Jaufré]. "Lanquan li jorn son lonc en mai." In *The Songs of Jaufré Rudel.* Edited and translated by Rupert T. Pickens. Toronto: Pontifical Institute of Medieval Studies, 1978.
Schulian, John, and others. *Xena: Warrior Princess.* Auckland, New Zealand: MCA Television, Renaissance Pictures, 1995-2001.
Sellstrom, A. Donald. *Corneille, Tasso and Modern Poetics.* Columbus: Ohio State University Press, 1986.
The Song of Roland. Edited by Gerard J. Brault. London and University Park: Pennsylvania State University Press, 1978.

The Song of Roland: Translations of the Versions in Assonance and Rhyme of the "Chanson de Roland." Translated by Joseph J. Duggan and Annalee C. Rejhon. Turnhout, Belgium: Brepols, 2012.
Tasso, Torquato. *Aminta*. Vinegia, Italy: [Aldus], 1581.
———. *Discorsi dell'arte poetica*. Venetia, Italy: Ad instanza di Giulio Vassalini, 1587.
———. *Gerusalemme liberata*. Casalmaggiore, Italy: Appresso Antonio Canacci, & Erasmo Viotti, 1581. 2nd ed. Edited by Bruno Maier. Milano: Rizzoli, 1988.
———. *Jerusalem Delivered: An English Prose Version*. Translated by Ralph Nash. Detroit: Wayne State University Press, 1987.
Tyson, Lois. *Critical Theory Today: A User-Friendly Guide*. 2nd ed. New York: Routledge, 2006.
U.S. Congress. *European Cooperation Act of 1948*. Public Law 80-472. 80th Cong., 2nd sess. (April 3, 1948): 137-59.
Vickers, Brian. "Leisure and Idleness in the Renaissance: the Ambivalence of Otium." *Renaissance Studies* 4, no. 2 (1990): 107-54.
Villon, François. *The Poems of François Villon*. Translated with notes by Galway Kinnell. New ed. London and Hanover, NH: University Press of New England, 1982.
"Warsaw Pact." "Treaty of Friendship, Co-operation, and Mutual Assistance…" May 14, 1955. *North Atlantic Treaty Organization* (NATO). Available online at http://avalon.law.yale.edu/20th_century/warsaw.asp (accessed May 15, 2016).
Weil, Simone. *The Need for Roots: Prelude to a Declaration of Duties Toward Mankind*. London: Routledge & Kegan Paul, 1952.
———. *La Pesanteur et la grâce*. Paris: Plon, 1947.
Wierzbicka, Anna. "Two languages, two cultures, one (?) Self: Between Polish and English." In *Translating Lives: Living with Two Languages and Cultures*, edited by Mary Besemeres and Anna Wierzbicka, 96-113. St Lucia: University of Queensland Press, 2007.
William IX, Duke of Aquitaine [Guilhen de Peitieu], "Farai un vers pos mi sonelh." In *Lark in the Morning: The Verses of the Troubadours. A Bilingual Edition.* Edited by Robert Kehew. Translated by Ezra Pound et al. Chicago: University of Chicago Press, 2005.
Wittgenstein, Ludwig. *Philosophical Investigations.* Translated by G.E.M. Anscombe. Oxford: Blackwell, 1953.

Index

African Americans, 51, 56, 88
Ariosto, Ludovico: *Orlando furioso*, 82–83
Aristotle: *Poetics*, 80–81, 82–83

Bakhtin, Mikhail: *Rabelais and His World*, 80
Balzac, Honoré de: *Le Père Goriot*, 5–6
Baudelaire, Charles: "L'Invitation au voyage", 67–68
Benedict XVI (pope), xiii
Berkeley: city of, 68–69. *See also* United States, University of California
Bernanos, Georges: *The Diary of a Country Priest*, 41

Calderón de la Barca, Pedro, 64
Camus, Albert, 50; *L'Étranger*, 27; *La Peste*, 5
Catholic (-ism). *See* Poland; United States
Cave, Terence: *The Cornucopian Text*, 80
Claudel, Paul: *L'Annonce faite à Marie*, 41
Cocteau, Jean, 6
Cohen, Baron: *Borat*, 80
Corneille, Pierre, 80–81, 87–93; *Le Cid*, 90; *Horace*, 84, 88–89; *Polyeucte*, 92–93
Czechoslovakia, 29, 73

Dąbrowska, Maria: *Noce i dnie* [*Nights and Days*], 75

Dante [Dante Alighieri]: *Divine Comedy*, 31
Derrida, Jacques, 97
Diderot, Denis: *Les Bijoux indiscrets*, 62
Dostoevsky, Fyodor: *The Eternal Husband*, 41
Duval, Edwin: *The Design of Rabelais's Pantagruel*, 79

Ecole Normale Supérieure at Saint-Cloud, 16

Fabliaux, 72
Flaubert, Gustave: *Bouvard et Pécuchet*, 34, 35, 36
France: *carte de séjour*, 29, 31; Grenoble, 17, 18–19; Latin Quarter, 22, 26, 68; Montmartre, 21; Nice, 18, 19; *Paris Match*, 5, 19; Préfecture of Nanterre, 29; Préfecture of Paris, 29; Saint Louis de Gonzague, 45–48, 53, 99; L'Union nationale des étudiants de France – (UNEF), 29, 30; Université Paris-Sorbonne (Paris IV), 29, 33–36, 57; Versailles, 38–39

García Márquez, Gabriel: *One Hundred Years of Solitude*, 64
Gide, André: *Les Caves du Vatican*, 27; *L'Immoraliste*, 6

Has, Wojciech: *Saragossa Manuscript*, 68
Hemingway, Ernest: *The Sun Also Rises*, 51
Holy Bible: 1 Corinthians 14:1-5, 95; Luke 19:11-27, 71–72; Matthew 18:3, 25:14-30, 71–72

Institut Français in Kraków, 5, 6, 8
Iron Curtain, 3, 26, 97. *See also* Poland

Jagiellonian University. *See* Poland
Jarezulski, General, 26, 30
Jesuit(s), xiv, 44, 45, 47, 48, 53, 57, 68, 70, 81, 84, 85, 89, 92, 95–96, 99, 100
Jews (-ish), 2, 24–25, 50, 91

kharjas, 74
Kraków. *See* Poland
Krashen, Stephen: natural approach, 59
Kramsch, Claire: *The Multilingual Subject*, 23, 34
Kristeva, Julia, 34

Marshall Plan, 3
Marx (-ist; -ism), 31; ideology, 10, 24; political economy, 10, 16
Mauroy, Pierre, 45
Michaux, Henri: *La nuit remue*, 36, 39–40
Mitterrand, François: "Savary Bill", 45
Molière, 5, 89; *Dom Juan*, 40; *Le Misanthrope*, 38–39; *Tartuffe*, 6, 37–38
Montaigne, Michel de: "Au Lecteur", 61
Myślenice. *See* Poland

Nerval, Gérard de: *Les Chimères*, 17; *Les filles du feu*, 17–18

Oakland, Calif., 51, 55, 88, 95. *See also* Saint Patrick's; United States

Paris. *See* France
Plato (-nic), xiii, 52, 56, 67; *Phaedrus*, 60, 61; *Republic*, 87
Petrarch (Petrarca, Francesco): "Letter to Posterity", 76
Poland: Catholic (-ism), 7, 15, 24, 27, 28, 30, 50, 70; Jagiellonian University, 9–10; Kraków, 1–20; marshal law (December 13, 1981), 6; mentality, 4, 12, 20; messianism, 14; Myślenice, 2; occupation (Soviet), 2–3, 5, 7, 16, 19, 26, 30, 45, 49, 70, 80; police *Służba Bezpieczeństwa*, 3; post-World War II, 2–3
Presley, Elvis: "Lonesome Cowboy", 60
priest (-hood), xiii, 95–96. *See also* Jesuit (s)

Rabelais, François, 61; *Gargantua*, 61; *Pantagruel*, 61, 79–80
Racine, Jean: *Andromaque*, 14–15
Radio Free Europe, 7
Rudel, Joffré [Jaufré]: "distant love", 60

Saint Joseph the Worker, Berkeley, Calif., 70
Saint Louis de Gonzague (Petit Collège of), 45–53
Salle de Lecture. *See* Institut Français
San Francisco, 55–65. *See also* United States
San Quentin State Prison, 14
Solidarność [Solidarity], 3, 12, 26
Society of Jesus. *See* Jesuits
Song of Roland, 12, 75
Spain, 44, 51, 63–64, 65; Cadiz, 65; Costa Blanca, 44; Salamanca, 44

Tasso, Torquato: "The Allegory of the Poem", 83; *Aminta*, 83; *Discorsi dell'arte poetica*, 83; *Gerusalemme liberata [Jerusalem Delivered]*, 80, 82–87, 90, 91; notion of *altri diletti*, 83
troubadour poetry, 60, 76

United States: Catholic (-ism), 63, 69, 70, 95–96, 98; California (-n), 11, 14, 50, 51, 55, 56, 59, 62, 85, 88, 96; Gospel music, 50, 56; San Francisco State University, 55–65; University of California, Berkeley, 11, 42, 55–92, 95, 99

Villon, François: "Ballade des dames du temps jadis", 1; "Ballade des pendus", 13–14

Warsaw Pact, 20

Weil, Simone: *L'Enracinement, prélude à une déclaration des devoirs envers l'être humain* [The Need for Roots], 88; *La Pesanteur et la grâce* [Gravity and Grace], 50, 52, 87

Wenders, Wim: *The American Friend*, 51, 59
William IX of Poitiers, 76
Wittgenstein, Ludwig, 106n3

About the Author

Matthew J. Motyka, S.J. is Associate Professor of Romance Languages in the Department of Modern and Classical Languages at the University of San Francisco where he directs the French and Italian programs. He holds a doctorate in Romance Languages and Literatures from the University of California, Berkeley. He is a Jesuit priest, member of the California Province.

www.ingramcontent.com/pod-product-compliance
Lightning Source LLC
Chambersburg PA
CBHW021145230426
43667CB00005B/265